Contributions to Economics

More information about this series at http://www.springer.com/series/1262

Omer Javed

The Economic Impact of International Monetary Fund Programmes

Institutional Quality, Macroeconomic Stabilization and Economic Growth

Springer

Omer Javed
Lahore, Pakistan

ISSN 1431-1933 ISSN 2197-7178 (electronic)
Contributions to Economics
ISBN 978-3-319-29177-2 ISBN 978-3-319-29178-9 (eBook)
DOI 10.1007/978-3-319-29178-9

Library of Congress Control Number: 2016934927

Springer Cham Heidelberg New York Dordrecht London

Printed on acid-free paper

Springer International Publishing AG Switzerland is part of Springer Science+Business Media (www.springer.com)

To the pursuit of knowledge for bringing welfare

Foreword

Institutions are important to understand the economic growth and to explain their quality. The most relevant empirical studies of Acemoglu, Robinson, and Rodrik demonstrate this evidence and demonstrate an open field of research in this direction. This book deals with a range of topics that are important for both academics and policymakers alike and emphasizes that usefulness of economics is enhanced when orthodox thinking is augmented with the underlying heterodox assumptions of Institutional Economics, whereby (among revisiting other Neo-Classical assumptions) the existence of transaction costs is not only understood to be non-zero, feeding in turn into production costs, but where market, hybrid, and firm structures are all seen to be competing frameworks for reaching at minimized transaction costs. The book, making an applied research under this premise, has made a significant contribution in putting up a strong case for the IMF (International Monetary Fund) to mainstream institutional focus in its programmes and to revise the underlying Neo-Classical assumptions of its programmes in the light of Institutional Economics.

When the author first approached me in early 2012, with a request to supervise his research to explore the consequences of greater institutional focus on the performance of IMF programmes, given my long-term interest in political economy, heterodox economics, and public economics, I found a natural inclination to be a part of this exciting research project. Reasons for doing this were manyfold, which made all the more sense as the research progressed during the course of the PhD in Economics programme.

Firstly, research literature during the last few decades had been emphasizing a policy framework based on deeper institutional fundamentals. Secondly, resurgence of Institutional Economics as a mainstream economic discipline since the 1980s brought centre stage the positive consequence of institutions for economic growth for countries in general, but this development could not find much attention and focus in IMF programmes. This situation presented itself as an important 'missing link' in the wake of neutral impacts of IMF programme conditionalities on economic growth in recipient countries and therefore appeared to be a significant and relevant motivation behind the research project. Lastly, and more importantly, the author being a former economist at IMF's office in Pakistan (where he worked for some years before starting the PhD programme) showed relevant first-hand exposure to the nature, working, and evolution of IMF programmes and, therefore, reflected the much needed appropriate mix of relevant professional experience and sound economic knowledge (for example, his master's degree in Economics earlier from the University of York, United Kingdom). Subsequently, the doctoral thesis that came about was received exceedingly well by external evaluators and PhD defence examiners.

The book at hand is an amended form of the PhD thesis in Economics, whereby primarily a full section has been included in Chap. 4, which analyses the institutional situation in Pakistan from the perspective of Institutional Economics. Taking a large dataset of political and economic institutional variables from new Institutional Economics literature, for a panel of IMF member countries, in terms of subgroups as non-programme and programme countries, along with frequent or prolonged users of IMF resources, over three decades (1980–2009), the study explores the nature of role and relationship between significant institutional determinants and macroeconomic stability, and economic growth, while also illustrating it with the example of a frequent user in the shape of Pakistan. This research holds important results. It finds the consequence of improvement in institutional quality determinants to be positive for macroeconomic stability and economic growth in IMF programme countries. This makes the book an important read for economic policymakers and academicians in general and the ones working on IMF programmes in particular (in terms of both IMF staff and related country authorities). The results of this applied research, it is hoped, will help improve IMF programmes in terms of providing a greater understanding to formulate current and future programmes that are more cognizant of enhancing institutional determinants.

The book also puts focus on the prolonged users of IMF resources. Moreover, it illustrates this by making a counterfactual analysis in the shape of enhanced institutional focus of IMF programmes on the stability and growth of Pakistan. Overall, the book is quite timely as the world embarks on achieving Sustainable Development Goals agreed upon at United Nations last month, since a considerable number of developing countries are either programme countries or prolonged users of IMF resources, and policy recommendations of this book will provide useful prescriptions and food for thought for development economists and policymakers in reaching at context-specific targeted interventions to channelize the improving-institutions-causing positive consequences on macroeconomic stability and economic growth, for reducing poverty and laying stronger basis for sustained development.

Department of Economic Policy and World Economic Structure Rosa Nonell
Faculty of Economics and Business
University of Barcelona
Barcelona, Spain
October 25, 2015

Preface

This study is motivated by the overall poor performance of International Monetary Fund (IMF) programmes in recipient countries in terms of economic growth consequences and tries to explore the relevance of institutional determinants for economic growth in these programme countries. The analysis, at the same time, also takes into consideration the claim by New Institutional Economics (NIE) literature, which points out an overall positive consequence of institutional quality determinants on economic growth for countries in general.

While working at International Monetary Fund's Resident Representative Office in Pakistan (my home country), I got the opportunity to closely witness the working of IMF programmes and how the underlying programme assumptions, other country experience, and the role of country authorities impact their formulation. The issues involved pushed me to think deeply into the specific outcomes from such programmes and also created in me a motivation to analyse research literature on the impact of IMF programmes in general. At the same time, while there was talk about structural reforms in such programmes, coming from a developing country experience I found little mention and emphasis, both among country authorities and by the IMF, on understanding the impact of improvement in institutional quality on economic outcomes. This lack of focus motivated me to explore the link between institutional quality and economic impact of IMF programmes.

More than just academic inquisitiveness, the motivation to take up this project at the PhD level was mainly twofold. Firstly, global financial crisis of the recent past challenged conventional wisdom of Washington Consensus and Neo-Classical/Monetarist thought process. Secondly, fundamental economic issues that allowed Pakistan to experience stability and growth only transitorily, even after being a frequent user of IMF resources for many years, pointed towards deeper analysis, and to see how the situation could have been different if the negotiated IMF conditionalities focused more on improving institutional quality.

It may be pointed here that the major part of the book is my PhD thesis in Economics, titled, 'Essays on institutional quality, macroeconomic stabilization, and economic growth in International Monetary Fund member countries'.

The major inclusion outside of the thesis in this monograph/book is in the shape of institutional analysis of Pakistan from the perspective of NIE. I find this analysis, which required a lot of effort and thinking, to be novel in its own right generally, but particularly in the case of Pakistan. Overall, it is hoped that the book will be useful for policymakers at the IMF and in individual countries, especially developing countries (many of which have remained frequent users of IMF resources) like Pakistan, in revising their policies to make them more context specific and meaningfully understanding the important role institutions play for achieving stability and growth.

Acknowledgements

The book which is primarily an outcome of my work as PhD student at the University of Barcelona (Spain) is indebted primarily to the patient and profound support of my PhD advisor, Dr. Rosa Nonell. The overall support of the Dean of the Faculty of Economics and Business, Dr. Elisenda Paluzie, the Director of the PhD Programme, Dr. Elisabet Viladecans, and in administrative matters from Mr. Jordi Roca (among others) brought seriousness of purpose and comfort to the overall research environment. Moreover, family and friends provided much needed support at the personal level, especially the birth of my first child, my daughter Roshanay, who brought me immense happiness.

Contents

1 Introduction 1
1.1 The IMF and Its Changing Role 1
1.2 IMF Programmes and Their Consequence 2
1.3 New Institutional Economics and IMF Programmes 3
1.4 Motivation 5
References 5

2 Determinants of Institutional Quality: A Case Study of IMF Programme Countries 7
2.1 Introduction 7
2.2 Literature Review 9
2.3 Data and Methodology 11
2.3.1 Theoretical Design 11
2.3.2 Sample 12
2.3.3 Data and Variable Description 15
2.3.4 Econometric Methodology 17
2.4 Estimation and Results 18
2.4.1 Robustness Check 28
2.5 Conclusion 28
Appendix 29
References 33

3 Institutional Quality, Macroeconomic Stabilization and Economic Growth: A Case Study of IMF Programme Countries 37
3.1 Introduction 37
3.2 Literature Review 38
3.3 Data and Methodology 41
3.3.1 Theoretical Design 41
3.3.2 Sample 42
3.3.3 Data and Variable Description 43
3.3.4 Econometric Methodology 44

3.4 Estimation and Results 46
3.4.1 Robustness Check 61
3.5 Conclusion 62
Appendix 63
References 70

4 IMF Programmes and Institutional Quality Determinants: Economic Scenarios in Pakistan 73
4.1 Introduction 73
4.2 Literature Review 75
4.3 Institutional Analysis of Pakistan: A NIE Perspective 79
4.3.1 Tracing the Political Economy 79
4.3.2 Defining the Actors in the Political Economy 80
4.3.3 Challenging the Assumptions and Actions of Policy 84
4.3.4 Designing an Institutional Incentive Structure for Pakistan 94
4.3.5 Towards Optimal Governance Structures 99
4.4 Data and Methodology 101
4.4.1 Theoretical Design 101
4.4.2 Sample 103
4.4.3 Data and Variable Description 103
4.4.4 Econometric Methodology 104
4.5 Estimation and Results 107
4.5.1 VAR and Impulse Response Functions of Sub-indices of MII and KOF Index of Globalization 107
4.5.2 VAR and Impulse Response Functions of MII, Real GDP and KOF Index of Globalization 111
4.5.3 Simulations 112
4.6 Conclusion 114
Appendix 115
References 119

5 Concluding Remarks 121
References 124

List of Tables

Table 2.1	Prolonged users	13
Table 2.2	Dependent variable -EFI- programme countries	19
Table 2.3	Dependent variable -Polity II- programme countries	21
Table 2.4	Dependent variable -EFI- prolonged users	23
Table 2.5	Dependent variable -Polity II- prolonged users	25
Table 2.6	Dependent variable -EFI- all member countries	29
Table 2.7	Dependent variable -Polity II- all member countries	31
Table 3.1	Dependent variable -real GDP- prolonged users	47
Table 3.2	Dependent variable -real GDP- non-prolonged users	49
Table 3.3	Dependent variable-MII-prolonged users	51
Table 3.4	Dependent variable -MII- non-prolonged users	53
Table 3.5	Dependent variable -real GDP- prolonged users	55
Table 3.6	Dependent variable -real GDP- non-prolonged users	57
Table 3.7	Dependent variable -real GDP- prolonged and non-prolonged users, and non-programme countries	62
Table 3.8	Dependent variable -real GDP-non-programme countries	63
Table 3.9	Dependent variable -MII- non-programme countries	65
Table 3.10	Dependent variable -real GDP-non-programme countries	67
Table 3.11	Group-wise list of IMF member countries	69
Table 4.1	Results of ADF test	108
Table 4.2	Results of Johansen cointegration test	108
Table 4.3	VAR lag order selection criteria	109
Table 4.4	VAR residual serial correlation LM test	109
Table 4.5	VAR residual heteroskedasticity test	109
Table 4.6	Comparison of actual and historically simulated figures	113
Table 4.7	Comparison of actual and stochastically simulated figures	114
Table 4.8	Reduced form VAR estimates	115
Table 4.9	Structural VAR estimates	117

List of Figures

Fig. 4.1 VAR Simulations of KOF index of globalization on components of MII 110
Fig. 4.2 Impulse response functions 112

List of Abbreviations

AD	Aggregate Demand
ADF	Augmented Dickey–Fuller
AIC	Akaike Information Criterion
AS	Aggregate Supply
BD	Budget Deficit
BOP	Balance of Payments
CPI	Corruption Perception Index
EFF	Extended Fund Facility
EFI	Economic Freedom Index
EIQ	Economic Institutional Quality
ER	Exchange Rate
ERV	Exchange Rate Variability
ESAF	Enhanced Structural Adjustment Facility
FD	Fiscal Deficit
FPP	Financial Programming and Policies
GDP	Gross Domestic Product
GGGD	General Government Gross Debt
GMM	Generalized Method of Moments
ICRG	International Country Risk Guide
IEO	Independent Evaluation Office
IFS	International Financial Statistics
IMF	International Monetary Fund
INF	Inflation Rate
IQ	Institutional Quality
MI	Macroeconomic Instability
MII	Macroeconomic Instability Index
NCE	Neo-Classical Economics
NIE	New Institutional Economics
OIE	Original Institutional Economics
PD	Public Debt
PIQ	Political Institutional Quality

PRGF	Poverty Reduction and Growth Facility
PTS	Political Terror Scale
REER	Real Effective Exchange Rate
RGDP	Real Gross Domestic Product
SAF	Structural Adjustment Facility
SBP	State Bank of Pakistan
SD	Standard Deviation
SDR	Special Drawing Rights
SIC	Schwarz Information Criterion
SRO	Statutory Regulatory Order
SVAR	Structural Vector Autoregression
VAR	Vector Autoregression
VAT	Value-Added Tax
VECM	Vector Error Correction Model
WDI	World Development Indicators
WEO	World Economic Outlook
WGI	Worldwide Governance Indicators

About the Author

Omer Javed holds a PhD in Economics degree from the University of Barcelona (Spain). He previously completed his master's in economics from the University of York (United Kingdom) and earlier from Government College University Lahore (Pakistan). In his doctoral thesis, he focused on the frameworks and determinants of institutions and their impact on macroeconomic stability and economic growth in International Monetary Fund (IMF) member countries. In 2015, a research paper, related but not a part of his doctoral thesis, 'Institutional determinants: a case study of IMF programme and non-programme countries', was published as a chapter in the book, 'The Political Economy of Governance: Institutions, Political Performance and Elections' (Springer 2015). His work experience spans both the public and private sectors. Moreover, his work as an economist at the Resident Representative Office of IMF in Pakistan served as a strong motivation in his choice of specialization in the doctoral thesis.

Chapter 1
Introduction

Abstract IMF was borne out of the Articles of Agreement in 1945 at Bretton Woods, mainly to oversee that member countries adhered to the par value system. During the course of time, the role of IMF enhanced to correcting both BOP related issues and growth concerns. Research indicated that programme impacts on recipient countries were below par for both economic growth and macroeconomic stability, mainly as an outcome of greater thrust on the demand side of the economy, at the cost of neglecting the much needed supply side focus. NIE underlined the importance of acknowledging and reducing transaction costs, through revision of underlying Neo-Classical assumptions of IMF programmes, so that the important role institutions play in reaching improved growth and stability consequences is both understood and implemented.

1.1 The IMF and Its Changing Role

The 1930s saw the Great Depression, and the response of various countries like raising trade barriers and devaluing currencies (to boost exports) put cracks in the monetary cooperation internationally. To correct this trend and to ensure that oversight is kept for avoiding such happenings in the future, in 1945 at Bretton Woods (USA), International Monetary Fund (IMF; or simply the 'Fund') was formed. The Fund came into being through the Articles of Agreement,[1] which were signed in 1945, bringing IMF into formal existence.

IMF oversaw that the member countries adhered to the par value system or the Bretton Woods system, whereby members pivoted their currencies to US dollar, and only made adjustment in their pegged rates for correcting fundamental balance of payments (BOP) disequilibrium (Bird 2003). With the dissolution of the Bretton Woods system during 1968–1973,[2] the Fund's oversight role got limited in the presence of flexible exchange rate regime. Having said that IMF created an Oil Facility to deal with the issue of huge increase in oil prices in the early 1970s,

[1] http://www.imf.org/external/pubs/ft/aa/index.htm

[2] http://www.imf.org/external/about/histend.htm

O. Javed, *The Economic Impact of International Monetary Fund Programmes*,
Contributions to Economics, DOI 10.1007/978-3-319-29178-9_1

whereby through the Facility surplus oil related revenues of oil exporting countries were re-routed to oil importing countries to deal with balance of payments crisis in the oil importing countries. Surplus oil revenues also meant commercial banks had a large pool of loanable funds for countries in BOP crisis, but with the rising of floating exchange rates by the end of 1970s, meant interest payments became a problem for these countries (which included developing countries). The Third World debt crisis saw an increase in IMF's role who lent to these countries, under IMF programme. Although borrowing related conditionalities[3] were first introduced in early 1950s by IMF to address fears of United States due to its underwriting of Fund's operations, the role of conditionality enhanced with IMF's greater coverage of lending operations, in terms of more member countries helped in resolving their BOP crisis. Hence, it could be seen that the oversight role of the IMF, had enhanced to correcting BOP related issues (through Structural Adjustment Facility (SAF) in 1986), and correcting BOP related issues and enhancing economic growth through Enhanced Structural Adjustment Facility (ESAF).[4] Thus, the enhancement of scope meant that IMF's focus was now both macroeconomic issues and economic growth of recipient countries, apart from the primarily initial oversight role.

1.2 IMF Programmes and Their Consequence

The Third World debt crisis caused many developing countries in problem to turn away from private banks to IMF lending, which meant greater role for the IMF, and in turn greater scrutiny of IMF programmes. In fact, with the fall of Communism in early 1990s and the move of those countries towards market economy system, led to further increase in IMF's clientele, and for these countries a 'Systematic Transformation Facility' was created by the Fund (Killick 1995). According to Bird (2003) the design of the IMF programme came under criticism for tilting heavily on the side of the Monetarist way of thinking, since more focus was placed on the demand side of the economy, and less on the supply side, and in that sense the programme was too rigid to accommodate the specific needs of a particular country; and New Structuralists found the programme conditionalities to have stagflationary consequences for recipient countries. In fact the opening up of ESAF window (and previously of SAF facility), which was later renamed in 1999 to Poverty Reduction and Growth Facility (PRGF) due to expansion of Fund's role to poverty reduction, was a response by IMF to focus more on supply side- and microeconomic measures (Bird 1996).

[3] According to Barro and Lee (2005, p. 1248), the process whereby quarterly installments are released to programme countries when they meet a pre-decided set of performance benchmarks, is referred to as the process of conditionality.

[4] http://www.imf.org/external/np/exr/chron/chron.asp

Yet, the response of IMF to deal with the supply-side related criticism has remained below satisfaction. Although according to Schadler et al. (1993) internal observations of IMF considered this response to be positive, academics/researchers like Killick (1995) criticized IMF's underlying basis for reaching such a conclusion. In fact, an independent evaluation of ESAF by IMF was more critical than the earlier positive internal evaluations, but according to Botchwey et al. (1998) IMF only reluctantly and partially accepted the findings of the independent evaluators. The consequence of all this has been that overall during the last three decades or so, Fund programmes have not allowed recipient countries to achieve sustained macroeconomic stability (Evrensel 2002; Easterly 2005), and have at most been neutral for economic growth (Haque and Khan 1998; Bird 2001; Barro and Lee 2005; Bird 2007; Arpac et al. 2008).

1.3 New Institutional Economics and IMF Programmes

Williamson (1975) coined the term of 'New Institutional Economics' (NIE)[5] (Chavance 2009, p. 45). His approach was critical of Neo-Classical Economics (NCE), since it did not consider the importance of institutions, the underlying role of transaction cost[6] and firm (Chavance 2009, p. 45; Groenewegen et al. 2010, p. 65). NIE agrees with NCE that economic agents look to maximize their utility (or profit), but unlike the Neo-Classical and Monetarist schools of thought, they find the rationality of economic agents to be bounded in the wake of opportunistic behaviour and asymmetric information.

In such an environment, there will be costs associated firstly with reaching a price mechanism that truly reflects the buyers and sellers potential in markets and, secondly costs will be involved in successfully negotiating contracts among individual economic agents or groups (Chavance 2009, p. 45). Coase (1937, p. 388) pointed out that in case of high transaction costs, it may be more suitable for an economic agent to move away from the governance structure of a market to a governance structure of a firm, if the later helps the agent in economizing such costs better than the market. Institutions help evolve these governance structures that help coordinate markets and firms so that transaction costs could be optimally reduced (Chavance 2009) and in doing so (unlike Neo-Classical school of thought) give greater role to government, both for regulation and for directly involving themselves in markets and/or firms if need be, depending on a particular economy and given sector(s) within it. These specifications of NIE, therefore, also highlight

[5] NIE is in contrast to the Original Institutional Economics (OIE) school, which is mainly based on the works by such institutional economists as Thorstein Veblen (1857–1929) and John R. Commons (1862–1945) (Groenewegen et al. 2010, p. 64, 65 and 87).

[6] Transaction costs included costs related with gathering and inspecting information, along with pertaining to enforcement, among others (Dahlman 1979, p. 148).

the importance for reform policy formulation, which should not be one-size-fits-all, but should be 'context specific' depending on the particular nature, composition and requirement of an economy.

Institutions are therefore, seen as vital in dealing with opportunistic behaviour and information related costs (Groenewegen et al. 2010, pp. 13–24, 36–38). While Williamson sees institutions only in the nature of formal rules that formulate governance structures (in public and private realms and both for markets and firms, and their hybrid),[7] another important proponent of NIE, Douglass North considers them as composed of formal (written rules) and informal constraints (unwritten and communicated by society as social norms, behaviour, and culture) (Chavance 2009, p. 79; North 1990, p. 4, 37, 47). Hence, institutions in the shape of laws and conventions see greater role of government in realizing an environment where contracts are abided by, and property rights[8] are distributed and guarded adequately against any possible opportunistic behaviour. NIE points out that through institutions, different governance structures (within government and private sectors) are evolved that help reduce transaction costs. Through such governance structures, pricing mechanism in markets and firms are improved, costs are adequately reduced for negotiating and implementing contracts, and incentives and checks are put in place to help reduce inefficiencies in distribution and enforcement of property rights (Groenewegen et al. 2010, pp. 118–120). All this is expected to reduce transaction costs, which in turn feed into lowering overall production costs, incentivizing greater investment, and positively affecting economic growth.

Bird (2003, p. 5) indicated that IMF programmes were strongly influenced by the Monetarist thought process, whereby showing greater tilt towards the demand side of the economy rather that the supply side. Looking more deeply into the basic formulation of IMF programmes, Killick (1995, p. 129) indicates that the analytical framework of these programmes is based on the Polak Model (Polak 1957). As per this model, imbalance in balance of payments results from excessive creation of domestic credit over money (supply or) demand (usually resulting as a consequence of excessive financing of budget deficit). Bird (2003, p. 5) pointed out that traditional macroeconomic thinking-based conditionality in IMF programmes overlooked the important role of government as a 'crowding-in' factor (especially in the case of developing countries), and according to empirical evidence, programme assumptions produced little impact on macroeconomic variables in IMF programmes, on one hand, and as per New Structuralists resulted in stagflationary consequences for programme countries.

Both Neo-Classical and Monetarist schools of thought see virtually automatic clearing of markets, since they see a world where economic agents show no opportunistic behaviour, are rational and that the information they need to reach

[7] A hybrid is such a governance structure that is characterized by features of both the firm and market (Groenewegen et al. 2010, p. 125).

[8] Eggertsson (1996, p. 7) points out that Institutional Economics defines property rights as an actor's right to use assets that are valuable (Alchian 1965).

utility (or profit) maximizing (or cost minimizing) decisions entail no cost (Groenewegen et al. 2010, pp. 14–15). Hence, one sees limited role of government and institutions in the world of this traditional economic thinking. Since, IMF programmes borrow heavily from this traditional thinking, therefore, the conditionalities primarily focus on monetary aggregates targeting on the demand side of the economy, and have not concerned themselves much with institutions on the supply side of the economy. Empirical evidence, in particular, during the last three decade or so, indicates that institutions matter for economic growth (Groenewegen et al. 2010, pp. 36–38; Rodrik et al. 2002; Hall and Jones 1999; Acemoglu and Johnson 2005; Afonso and Jalles 2011). Although IMF has also internalized this role of institutions to some extent and has tried to evolve programmes to improve the focus on the supply side of the economy, but once again their over-indulgence in the traditional economic thinking, has not allowed them to move away to a reform agenda that understands the importance of improving determinants of institutional quality (IQ) in programme countries.

1.4 Motivation

NIE literature indicates institutions matter for economic growth. Empirical evidence of the last three decades or so indicates that countries which have focused reform agenda on improving institutional quality, have witnessed an overall positive impact of this on economic growth. This background motivates an analysis into understanding the role determinants of institutional quality play on economic growth in IMF programme countries. A positive consequence in this regard should underline the importance of institutions to IMF, so that their future programmes base themselves more on the NIE framework, something which it is hoped will help reverse the previously poor record of IMF programmes in terms of economic growth consequences. It may be indicated here that the in the book, both formal and informal aspects of institutions will be taken into account.

References

Acemoglu D, Johnson S (2005) Unbundling institutions. J Polit Econ 113:949–995

Afonso A, Jalles JT (2011) Economic performance and government size. ECB Working paper series No. 1399. ECB, Germany

Alchian AA (1965) Some economics of property rights. Il Politico 30:816–829

Arpac O, Bird G, Mandilaras A (2008) Stop interrupting: an empirical analysis of the implementation of IMF programs. World Dev 36:1493–1513

Barro RJ, Lee J (2005) IMF programs: who is chosen and what are the effects? J Monet Econ 52:1245–1269

Bird G (1996) Borrowing from the IMF: the policy implications of recent empirical research. World Dev 24:1753–1760

Bird G (2001) IMF Programs: do they work? Can they be made to work better? World Dev 29:1849–1865
Bird G (2003) The IMF and the future: issues and options facing the fund, 1st edn. Routledge, London
Bird G (2007) The IMF: a bird's eye view of its role and operations. J Econ Surv 21:683–745
Botchwey K, Collier P, Gunning JW, Hamada K (1998) Report by a group of independent experts: external evaluation of ESAF. IMF, Washington, DC
Chavance B (2009) Institutional economics, 1st edn. Routledge, London. Originally published in French, Paris (2007)
Coase R (1937) The nature of the firm. Economica 4:386–405
Dahlman CJ (1979) The problem of externality. J Law Econ 22:141–162
Easterly W (2005) What did structural adjustment adjust? The association of policies and growth with repeated IMF and World Bank adjustment loans. J Dev Econ 76:1–22
Eggertsson T (1996) A note on the economics of institutions. In: Alston LJ, Eggertsson T, North DC (eds) Empirical studies in institutional change, 1st edn. Cambridge University Press, Cambridge, pp 6–24
Evrensel AY (2002) Effectiveness of IMF-supported stabilization programmes in developing countries. J Int Money Finance 21:565–587
Groenewegen J, Spithoven A, van den Berg A (2010) Institutional economics: an introduction, 1st edn. Palgrave Macmillan, Hampshire
Hall RE, Jones CI (1999) Why do some countries produce so much more output per worker than others? Q J Econ 114:83–116
Killick T (1995) IMF programmes in developing countries: design and effects, 1st edn. Routledge, London
North D (1990) Institutions, institutional change, and economic performance, 1st edn. Cambridge University Press, New York, NY
Polak JJ (1957) Monetary analysis of income formation and payments problems. IMF staff papers, vol 6. IMF, Washington, DC, pp 1–50
Rodrik D, Subramanian A, Trebbi F (2002) Institutions rule: the primacy of institutions over geography and integration in economic development. Centre for Economic Policy Research Discussion paper series no 3643. Centre for Economic Policy Research, London
Schadler S, Rozwadowski F, Timari S, Robinson DO (1993) Economic adjustment in low income countries: experience under the enhanced structural adjustment facility. IMF Occasional paper no. 106. IMF, Washington, DC
Ul Haque N, Khan MS (1998) Do IMF-supported programs work? A survey of the cross-country empirical evidence. IMF working paper no. 98/169. IMF, Washington, DC
Williamson OE (1975) Markets and hierarchies. Analysis and antitrust implications, 1st edn. Free Press, New York, NY

Chapter 2
Determinants of Institutional Quality: A Case Study of IMF Programme Countries

Abstract Taking a panel data of IMF member countries, this chapter primarily focuses on the IMF programme countries, during 1980–2009; a time period during which the number of IMF programmes witnessed an increasing trend. Firstly, important determinants of economic- and political institutional quality in IMF programme countries are estimated by applying the System-GMM approach, so as to find significant determinants among them. Here, a parliamentary form of government, aggregate governance level, civil liberties, openness, and property rights all enhance overall institutional quality. Specifically, greater monetary- and investment freedom are conducive for political institutional quality, while military in power impacts negatively. Moreover, economic growth is conducive for enhancing economic institutional quality.

2.1 Introduction[1]

The effectiveness of the conditionalities of IMF programmes (mostly restricted to addressing macroeconomic stability concerns) on recipient countries has come under severe criticism, especially in terms of their consequence for economic growth (IEO 2007[2]; Bird and Willett 2004), something that the IMF has also realized along the way (IMF 2005a; IEO 2007).

Notwithstanding the level of implementation of IMF programmes by recipient countries (an area that is still under-researched), research has shown mostly a neutral or negative program impact on economic growth; and to look beyond the NCE underlying basis of these programmes (Kuncic 2014). Such behavioural

[1] There are two earlier versions of this paper placed at 'Munich Personal RePEc Archive'. First version placed on November 11, 2013 (https://mpra.ub.uni-muenchen.de/51344/); second on June 3, 2014 (https://mpra.ub.uni-muenchen.de/51409/)

[2] Independent Evaluation Office (IEO).

O. Javed, *The Economic Impact of International Monetary Fund Programmes*, Contributions to Economics, DOI 10.1007/978-3-319-29178-9_2

assumptions consider a zero-transaction cost[3] world, and therefore do not see much role of institutions, which according to NIE are instrumental in reducing the costs involved, incentivize private property protection, innovation and investment, and in turn help boost economic growth.

Given this background, Kuncic (2014), for example, advocated the adoption of NIE framework for analyzing the dynamics and consequences of social (and other) interactions among economic agents. Moreover, most empirical research conducted from 1995 to 2004 pointed towards the presence of significant relation between IQ and economic performance (Ugur 2010).

The current study aims to find out significant institutional quality determinants, in the light of NIE framework, in programme countries of IMF (countries that have been under an IMF programme at one time or the other), with the aim to influence IMF in enhancing the scope of its future programmes by considerably increasing focus on institutional determinants; which is likely to result in an improved impact of such programmes on economic growth of programme countries.

Furthermore, the study also intends to focus on prolonged users[4] (member countries that have been under the IMF programmes for longer periods of time) as a sub-group, whose numbers have increased over the years since the breakdown of the Bretton Woods system (Barro and Lee 2005; IEO 2002). Here also, the intention is to reach at determinants of institutional quality that are significant. Focus on the prolonged users is all the more necessary, since there is a rising concern (in terms of moral hazard issue) that such countries have under-performed in terms of carrying out hard economic reforms at the back of relatively easily available IMF resources (Evrensel 2002).

Hence, all IMF member countries (188 to be precise[5]) have been taken, along with the two sub-groups, namely programme countries, and prolonged users. Time period under review is from 1980 (when the role and penetration of IMF programmes increased) to 2009.

The structure of the study is as follows: Sect. 2.2 reviews important related literature on the topic under discussion, data and methodology are discussed in Sect. 2.3, while estimation and results are focused upon in Sect. 2.4. The last section (which is Sect. 2.5) concludes the study.

[3] Asymmetric information and heterogeneous nature of individual perceptions about how the world works, means transactions have associated costs; which are reduced by institutions (Harriss et al. 1995; North 1994, p. 17).

[4] According to IEO (2002, p. 9 and 24) countries fall in the prolonged user category if they remain under an IMF programme for at least 7 years in a decade.

[5] Complete list at: https://www.imf.org/external/np/sec/memdir/memdate.htm

2.2 Literature Review

Literature sees IMF's financial programming techniques to be of the nature of over-simplistic/ one-size-fits-all, asking in turn to revisit the underlying basis of programmes (Buira 1983; Bird 2001; Bird 2007). Such an inflexible nature is therefore unsuitable for the varied nature of programme countries (Stiglitz 2001; Vreeland 2006; Abbott et al. 2010), which proves to be too conventional and rigid specifically for the developing countries, and remains a reason for neutral impact on economic growth (Abbott et al. 2010).

In the same vein, Nsouli et al. (2004) found absence of focus on institutional enhancing factors in evaluating programme success rate; furthermore indicated better institutional quality and conducive political environment had positive consequences for macroeconomic outcomes, and programme implementation rates. Similarly, Arpac et al. (2008) conducted a study covering 95 countries and a time period of 1992–2004 to point out that programme implementation record was better where countries had more trade openness (in turn, a significant institutional determinant). Also, the study suggested to IMF to focus on domestic politics also while forming expectations about the extent of programme implementation in a country.

Importance of institutions has been underlined for a long time. Adam Smith (1976, p. 910)[6] showed interest in institutions when he highlighted that a good judicial system (in other words, rule of law, which is an important institutional factor) was a pre-requisite for economic activity. Furthermore, he pointed out that the underlying differences between countries and regions were explained by institutional factors (Smith 1976, p. 405).

Sadly, NCE forgot this initial understanding by ignoring institutions. Rather it assumed a free-market, perfect competition basis for Pareto optimality or efficiency[7] and took a production function that included labour and capital (Ugur 2010). Such a technical production function is incompatible with regard to the existence of property rights and efficient contract enforcement (Rodrik 2000), and does not explain the difference between developing and developed world (Ugur 2010).

Attention on the significance of institutions was later on re-emphasized in the decade of 1980s,[8] and especially during the 1990s from lessons obtained from the liberalization reform. Hence, it was realized that institutions were required for incentive system of price signal to work for increasing national welfare (Rodrik 2000), and that they channelized investment away from rent-seeking behaviour to one that promoted creativity, and greater production (Shirley 2008). It was also pointed out that small changes at the margins helped improve economic growth

[6] Adam Smith's book, 'An Inquiry into the Nature and Causes of the Wealth of Nations' was originally published in 1776.

[7] In such a situation, welfare of one person can only be increased by decreasing someone else's welfare (Groenewegen et al. 2010, p. 16).

[8] By Kormendi and Meguire (1985), and Scully (1988), Ugur (2010, p. 9).

(Rodrik 2005). At the same time it was highlighted that while traditionally, institutional change has been seen to happen gradually, it was nevertheless not the only way for such a change to take place, but rather also at a revolutionary pace as for example was demonstrated by East Asian economies (Quibria 2002).

Shirley (2008) highlighted that NIE literature identified four sources for institutions being underdeveloped. Firstly, a legacy of poor institutions from colonizers, and which in turn needed to be set right as one of the complementing ways to enhance macroeconomic stability (North 1990; La Porta et al. 1997; Acemoglu et al. 2001a, 2003). Secondly, on the contrary where the country had endowments, colonizers did develop institutions to extract from local resources. Moreover, there also existed a positive relation between institutional development and the extent of settlement of colonizer (which in turn relied on the level of livability of colonizers locally); that is, the higher the extent of such a settlement, the greater the level of institutional development, as could be seen in the case of Australia or Canada for that matter, among others (Acemoglu et al. 2001a, b; Acemoglu and Robinson 2012).

Thirdly, lack of political competition outside and inside of the country resulted in little motivation for leaders to build institutions for peoples' benefit at large, where such leaders faced virtually no strong opposition for building institutions that served their own vested interests (Nugent and Robinson 2002). Fourthly, (at times) certain beliefs and norms discouraged development of markets and institutions (North 1994, 2005; Knack and Keefer 1997). Moreover, North (1990, p. 110) indicated that the institutional incentive system of the developing countries did not induce productive activity, and that is the underlying reason for the level of poverty there (being on the higher side).

Many studies have pointed out the important role played by improvement in institutional quality in enhancing economic growth (for example, Rodrik et al. 2002; Hall and Jones 1999). Specifically, Acemoglu and Johnson (2005, p. 953) pointed out that income per capita was substantially higher in those countries, as compared to others, where institutions protected property rights more (a similar result highlighted by Afonso and Jalles (2011)).

Political- and economic institutions are the two main types of institutions (IMF 2005b; Joskow 2008; Kuncic 2014), where the former mainly encompass political environment/agents (for example, rules of elections, voters, extent and nature of power of government, etc.), while the later constitute the environment that enable functioning of markets (for instance, property rights). Moreover, 'inclusive economic institutions' work towards enhancing participation of people in economic activity through provision of better protection of property rights and other institutional determinants of a facilitating environment, as against 'extractive economic institutions', which transferred resources from the many to the group(s) that forms this collusion (to benefit it, in turn); furthermore, an inclusive/extractive economic institution resulted because of an inclusive/extractive political institutional setup (Acemoglu and Robinson 2012, pp. 74–82; Acemoglu 2006; Acemoglu and Robinson 2008).

2.3 Data and Methodology

2.3.1 Theoretical Design

The present study is based on NIE's methodological framework, in which institutions are an outcome of rules and regulations that human beings establish, to act as constraints for governing the way humans deal with each other (North 1990, p. 3). According to Williamson (1975) interaction takes place in either markets, firms, or their hybrid,[9] while the choice of a particular governance structure, in this regard, depends where the transaction costs are getting minimized the most (Chavance 2009, p. 45 and 46; Groenewegen et al. 2010, pp. 123–125). Institutions encompass both formal and informal constraints that shape the way humans interact (North 1990, p. 4), where the former are composed of written rules (pertaining to politics, economy, and contracts, among others; North 1990, p. 47), while the later depict the unwritten (and communicated by society) social norms, behaviour, and culture (North, 1990, p. 4 and 37). While Williamson (1975) only considers formal rules, North (1990) considers both formal and informal constraints. In this study, both formal and informal aspects of institutions will be taken into account.

According to North (1990, p. 4 and 5) while institutions are the rules, which govern the game, the agents who play the game are called organizations. These evolve as a consequence of a particular institutional framework, and in turn, influence that institutional framework; hence, both institutions and organizations interact to bring institutional change. Also, North (1994, p. 5) points out that institutional change is a result of choices that are in turn influenced by the changes that happen externally (outside a particular society or system), and the learning that takes place internally (within a society or system).

While costs involved in personal exchange are reduced by traders through relying on private means (Williamson 1985), and through trust and cooperation (Knack and Keefer 1997), impersonal exchange requires in addition, enforcement mechanisms implemented by state (Milgrom et al. 1990). Similarly, Coase (1992, p. 197) emphasized the importance of lowering transaction costs for fostering exchange in the economy. Positive institutional change, therefore, means improvement in institutional quality, eventually leading to economic growth.

According to NIE literature, institutions are both political and economic, where one influences the other to bring overall change in institutional quality (Acemoglu 2006; Acemoglu and Robinson 2008; Acemoglu and Robinson 2012). Therefore, the current study analyzes institutional quality in terms of economic- and political institutional quality (in line with for example IMF 2005b), in an effort to find out significant political/governance-, and economic institutional determinants for enhancing overall institutional quality in IMF programme countries. In the wake of NIE literature that supports the flow of positive causation from improvement in

[9] A hybrid is such a governance structure that is characterized by features of both the firm and market (Groenewegen et al. 2010, p. 125).

institutional quality to economic growth (Ugur 2010), and in the light of criticism of previous IMF programmes in terms of their lack of consequence for economic growth (IEO 2007; Bird and Willett 2004), such a conclusion is supposed to help IMF make necessary adjustments in its FPP to enhance focus on determinants of institutional quality.

2.3.2 *Sample*

While overall IMF member countries stand at 188,[10] the sample is composed of 129 'programme countries', which are those that have adopted at least one IMF programme during 1980–2009.[11] The reason behind taking this sample in the first place, is based on the premise that one of the main reasons why IMF programmes have under-performed in terms of their impact on economic growth, is due to their insufficient focus on improving institutional quality (an area, which has been shown in NIE literature to have positive consequences for economic growth).

Prolonged Users As an extension, the sample of prolonged users has also been taken to analyze, in particular, significant institutional determinants in these countries (for the same time period). Hence, during 1980–2009, around one-third of them (44 to be precise) were prolonged users [listed in Table 2.1 in descending order of number of years under IMF programme(s)]. Hence, Mali and Senegal have been the most prolonged users, having each been under an IMF programme(s) for a total of 23 years overall in the sample period. Geographical mapping indicates that almost half of the prolonged users belonged to the continent of Africa, followed by Asia (at around one-fifth of the total prolonged users); places that have otherwise also seen prevalence of absolute poverty on the higher side. This, in turn, opens up possible areas for future research, to understand the consequences of IMF resources for poverty and the overall economy, for prolonged users of these two continents.

Further analysis of Table 2.1 indicates that during the decade of 1980s there were surprisingly no prolonged users. At the same time, the next two decades of 1990s and 2000s, respectively, saw a mushrooming of prolonged users (28 countries to be precise, falling under this category, in each decade). Moreover, it could be seen that 12 countries remained prolonged users in both the 1990s and 2000s; pointing towards a possible prolonged user syndrome through the likely existence of moral hazard, whereby countries may have relied more on IMF resources than going for hard economic reforms.

[10] Complete list of IMF member countries is at: http://www.imf.org/external/country/index.htm

[11] Information on whether a country has been under IMF program or not has been taken from IMF website (http://www.imf.org/external/np/fin/tad/exfin1.aspx).

Table 2.1 Prolonged users

		Years under IMF programme					Prolonged user (yes/no)			
Sr.#	Country name	1980–1989	1990–1999	2000–2009	Total	Continent	1980–1989	1990–1999	2000–2009	1990–2009
1	Mali	4	9	10	23	Africa	0	1	1	1
2	Senegal	6	8	9	23	Africa	0	1	1	1
3	Mexico	6	5	10	21	N. America	0	0	1	0
4	Mozambique	3	9	9	21	Africa	0	1	1	1
5	Niger	6	5	10	21	Africa	0	0	1	0
6	Madagascar	6	5	9	20	Africa	0	0	1	0
7	Malawi	4	8	7	19	Africa	0	1	1	1
8	Mauritania	5	8	6	19	Africa	0	1	0	0
9	Tanzania	3	7	9	19	Africa	0	1	1	1
10	Uganda	3	9	7	19	Africa	0	1	1	1
11	Benin	1	7	10	18	Africa	0	1	1	1
12	Burkina Faso	0	8	10	18	Africa	0	1	1	1
13	Cameroon	2	7	9	18	Africa	0	1	1	1
14	Albania	0	7	10	17	Europe	0	1	1	1
15	Argentina	5	8	4	17	S. America	0	1	0	0
16	Bolivia	3	9	5	17	S. America	0	1	0	0
17	Kyrgyz Republic	0	7	10	17	Asia	0	1	1	1
18	Guyana	0	10	6	16	S. America	0	1	0	0
19	Sierra Leone	1	6	9	16	Africa	0	0	1	0
20	Armenia	0	6	9	15	Europe	0	0	1	0
21	Chad	3	7	5	15	Africa	0	1	0	0
22	Pakistan	1	7	7	15	Asia	0	1	1	1
23	Rwanda	0	5	10	15	Africa	0	0	1	0
24	Georgia	0	6	8	14	Europe	0	0	1	0

(continued)

Table 2.1 (continued)

Sr.#	Country name	Years under IMF programme				Continent	Prolonged user (yes/no)			
		1980–1989	1990–1999	2000–2009	Total		1980–1989	1990–1999	2000–2009	1990–2009
25	Guinea	3	7	4	14	Africa	0	1	0	0
26	Philippines	6	7	1	14	Asia	0	1	0	0
27	Zambia	2	3	9	14	Africa	0	0	1	0
28	Bulgaria	0	8	5	13	Europe	0	1	0	0
29	Burundi	3	2	8	13	Africa	0	0	1	0
30	Dominican Republic	2	4	7	13	N. America	0	0	1	0
31	Ghana	0	5	8	13	Africa	0	0	1	0
32	Jordan	2	8	3	13	Asia	0	1	0	0
33	Turkey	1	3	9	13	Asia	0	0	1	0
34	Dominica	5	0	7	12	N. America	0	0	1	0
35	Honduras	0	7	5	12	N. America	0	1	0	0
36	Nicaragua	0	4	8	12	N. America	0	0	1	0
37	Tajikistan	0	4	8	12	Asia	0	0	1	0
38	Lao	1	7	3	11	Asia	0	1	0	0
39	Macedonia	0	7	4	11	Europe	0	1	0	0
40	Panama	4	7	0	11	N. America	0	1	0	0
41	Mongolia	0	7	3	10	Asia	0	1	0	0
42	Serbia	0	1	8	9	Europe	0	0	1	0
43	Algeria	1	7	0	8	Africa	0	1	0	0
44	Russian Fed.	0	7	0	7	Asia	0	1	0	0
Total							0	28	28	12

Note: A prolonged user is represented by 1, and 0 otherwise; indicated under prolonged user heading above

2.3.3 *Data and Variable Description*

Economic Institutional Quality (EIQ) Following IMF (2005b), EIQ will be measured by using the proxy of Economic Freedom Index (EFI) of the Cato Institute,[12] which captures five aspects of government size, the makeup of the legal framework and the extent of protection of property rights, along with access to sound money, the level of liberty to trade internationally, and business, labour, and credit rules and regulations. Data is taken from 1980 to 2009 (5-yearly up till 2000, and yearly after that). Ahmadov et al. (2013) also employed EFI by Gwartney and Lawson (2003). The reason for employing this economic institutional proxy is the larger diversity of aspects that it includes, than some of the other proxy variables that have been used in previous studies like Investment Profile (International Country Risk Guide; ICRG), and Freedom of the Press: Economic Environment (Freedom House).

Political Institutional Quality (PIQ) This will be measured using the proxy of Polity II (from the Polity IV dataset of Marshall et al. 2011), which captures 'political structures and regime change'.[13] This proxy has been taken (like for example by Afonso and Jalles 2011) to indicate, which variables significantly determine political institutional quality.[14] Data is taken for the time period 1980–2009. This has been preferred due to the larger extent of its coverage of political environment, than some of the other political institutional proxy variables that have been used in earlier research like Democratic Accountability (ICRG), Corruption Perception Index (CPI; Transparency International), and Political Terror Scale (PTS).[15]

Political/Governance Variables A host of variables are taken from the Database of Political Institutions,[16] to overall see the impact of electoral rules and political system. Variables analysed here include, (i) regime (is a dummy variable indicating 0 for presidential, and 1 for parliamentary form of government; also taken in the study by Afonso and Jalles 2011), (ii) military (chief executive a military officer or not; existence of it is represented by 1, 0 otherwise), (iii) Herfindahl Index Government (to basically reflect the strength/proportion of government seats in parliament), and (iv) Herfindahl Index Opposition (indicates the extent of representation of opposition in parliament).

---

[12] http://www.cato.org/economic-freedom-world

[13] http://www.icpsr.umich.edu/icpsrweb/ICPSR/studies/9263?q=PolityIIandsearchSource=icpsr-landing

[14] http://www.systemicpeace.org/inscr/inscr.htm

[15] http://www.politicalterrorscale.org/

[16] http://econ.worldbank.org/WBSITE/EXTERNAL/EXTDEC/EXTRESEARCH/0,,contentMDK:20649465~pagePK:64214825~piPK:64214943~theSitePK:469382,00.html

An aggregate governance indicator has also been included in the study as a regressor. This has been calculated as a simple average of the five indicators. These five variables are from Worldwide Governance Indicators (WGI; World Bank),[17] which, in turn, have been produced by Kaufmann et al. (2010).[18] These five indicators cover aspects with regard to the level of voice and accountability (found significant in IMF 2005b, for improving institutions), effectiveness of government, the situation of rule of law, the quality of regulations, and the extent of control of corruption.

Data on civil liberties is taken from Freedom in the World (publication of Freedom House).[19] Here, the least rating of degree of freedom is indicated by 1, while the highest rating is represented by 7.

Economic Variables The first regressor here is openness, and a broad proxy that has been used here is KOF Index of Globalization.[20] Data is taken for the available time period of 1980–2009. Openness is indicated in literature to be positively related with enhancing IQ (Rodrik et al. 2002; IMF 2005b). Although Alonso and Garcimartin (2013) did not find the impact of openness to be significant, KOF Index of Globalization, but due to its multidimensional approach, this has been included in the current study for checking for its possible significance.

Measures of economic freedom and prosperity are taken from the Index of Economic Freedom[21] to see their influence on institutional quality. Sub-indices taken here are, monetary-, fiscal-, and investment freedom, along with property rights. Unfortunately, data is only available since 1995; data is taken up till 2009.

Lastly, log real GDP (at constant 2005 US$; and taken from World Development Indicators (WDI)[22]) has been included in the study, as one of the regressors to see its impact on both economic- and political institutional quality.

Endogeneity NIE literature highlights the presence of the endogeneity issue in the case of institutions (for example Acemoglu et al. 2001a). In the current study, variables that are expected to be affected by this issue include property rights, aggregate governance indicator, fiscal freedom, monetary freedom, and real GDP for overall IQ. At the same time, variables expected to have endogeneity issue with respect to EIQ include investment freedom and KOF index of globalization; while civil liberties in the case of PIQ. Moreover, as lagged dependent variable is correlated with the error term, therefore, lagged EFI and lagged Polity II may cause endogeneity problem in the regression.

---

[17] http://data.worldbank.org/data-catalog/worldwide-governance-indicators

[18] http://info.worldbank.org/governance/wgi/index.aspx#home

[19] http://www.freedomhouse.org/report-types/freedom-world

[20] http://globalization.kof.ethz.ch/

[21] http://www.heritage.org/index/explore

[22] http://data.worldbank.org/data-catalog/world-development-indicators

2.3.4 *Econometric Methodology*[23]

IQ will be determined using the following basic model:

$$IQ_{it} = f\left(IQ_{i,t-1}, X_{it}, Z_{it}\right) + \omega_{it} \qquad (2.1)$$

where, institutional quality is indicated by IQ_{it}, lag of the dependent variable indicated by $IQ_{i,t-1}$, and variables with regard to political/governance aspects by the vector of X_{it}. Moreover, economic variables are indicated by the vector of Z_{it}; error term by ω_{it}.

While Eq. (2.1) gives the overall framework, the next two equations with regard to economic- and political institutional quality, respectively, are:

$$EIQ_{it} = \beta_i + \beta_1 EIQ_{i,t-1} + \beta_2 X_{it} + \beta_3 Z_{it} + \xi_t + \rho_{it} \qquad (2.2)$$

$$PIQ_{it} = \gamma_i + \gamma_1 PIQ_{i,t-1} + \gamma_2 X_{it} + \gamma_3 Z_{it} + \phi_t + \varphi_{it} \qquad (2.3)$$

where in the two equations above, country-fixed effects are indicated by β_i and γ_i, and time specific effects by ξ_t and ϕ_t; while the error-terms by ρ_{it} and φ_{it}.

Moreover, Eqs. (2.2) and (2.3) have been transformed by taking the first differences, as indicated below:

$$\Delta EIQ_{it} = \alpha_1 \Delta EIQ_{i,t-1} + \alpha_2 \Delta X_{it} + \alpha_3 \Delta Z_{it} + \theta_t + \varepsilon_{it} \qquad (2.4)$$

$$\Delta PIQ_{it} = \Omega_1 \Delta PIQ_{i,t-1} + \Omega_2 \Delta X_{it} + \Omega_3 \Delta Z_{it} + \tau_t + \sigma_{it} \qquad (2.5)$$

where Δ stands for change between years t and $t-1$ for a variable. At the same time, one set of year indicators each is represented by θ_t and τ_t, respectively. Furthermore, ε_{it} and σ_{it} respectively, are the error terms. It may be noted here that through these transformed models, the possibility of heterogeneity (which is not fully captured by the regressors) is successfully dealt with by the effective elimination of country-fixed effects.

The transformed models above [that is Eqs. (2.4) and (2.5)] have been estimated in the current study by Arellano and Bover (1995) approach. This approach has the advantage that it allows information in the equations to be simultaneously incorporated in both levels and difference forms.

At the same time, it is important to point out that inclusion of the lag dependent variable gives way to a statistical problem, by virtue of the lag dependent variable and the error term being automatically correlated with each other. Hence, the way out of this calls for including further lags of the dependent variable, which in turn act as instruments. Arellano and Bover (1995), and Blundell and Bond (1998) recommended for such model the GMM (Generalized Method of Moments)

[23] Similar discussion/details of the methodology section can be seen from Javed (2015).

approach.[24] Under this, the model gets estimated through GMM in both level and difference simultaneously; in turn further enhancing the efficiency of the model through the addition of even more instruments to the system. Furthermore, the current study employs standard errors that are completely robust towards serial correlation and arbitrary heteroskedasticity in GMM estimation. The above system has been estimated through the Stata software[25]; using the Stata command called 'xtabond2', which was developed by Roodman (2009).

2.4 Estimation and Results

Determinants of institutional quality have been estimated for both the economic institutional quality, and the political institutional quality. As indicated earlier, Economic Freedom Index and Polity II index have been used as proxies for these two, respectively. Also, while the main thrust of the estimation is on programme countries, focus has also been extended for prolonged users, as a special case. Tables 2.2 and 2.3 highlight the significant determinants of economic- and political institutional quality of the countries that have remained under IMF programme at one time or the other, during the sample period (that is, programme countries). Moreover, Tables 2.4 and 2.5 estimate the significant determinants of economic- and political institutional quality with regard to prolonged users.

To start with, it will be pertinent to indicate that the entire specifications pass the test of Hansen-J statistic, which is concerned with Over-Identifying Restrictions (OIR; Hansen 1982); bringing in turn validity to the instruments at hand. Further support of the specification of the models is obtained from meeting both the F-test for the overall significance of the regression, and the Arellano-Bond tests for serial correlation. Moreover, the reported OIR test points out that all the instruments are exogenous.[26]

The lag of both EIQ and PIQ remain positively significant for both programme countries and prolonged users, indicating high persistence in the evolution of IQ. This is in line with the path dependent nature of institutional evolution, where the past institutional setup feeds into the present; and forms an underlying reason for adopting the dynamic process in the current study.

The dummy variable, regime, indicates whether a country has parliamentary or a presidential form of government. The estimations indicate that regime is significantly positive throughout, which means that parliamentary form of government enhances both EIQ and PIQ in programme countries, as well as prolonged users.

The impact of the chief executive being a military personal is next estimated. It can be seen from the estimation that, military (in power) significantly and

[24] The work was originally done by Arellano and Bond (1991). This was taken forward by Arellano and Bover (1995), while Blundell and Bond (1998) extended it further.

[25] http://www.stata.com/

[26] Roodman (2007) provides details.

Table 2.2 Dependent variable -EFI- programme countries

Variables	(1)	(2)	(3)	(4)	(5)	(6)	(7)	(8)	(9)	(10)
Lag EFI	0.824***	0.921***	0.818***	0.845***	0.773***	0.509***	0.875***	0.836***	0.747***	0.496***
	(0.0696)	(0.0499)	(0.0585)	(0.0578)	(0.0403)	(0.0595)	(0.0620)	(0.0343)	(0.0397)	(0.0389)
Regime	0.348***									0.164
	(0.0923)									(0.118)
Military	−0.0160									0.0122
	(0.111)									(0.166)
Herf. Index Opp.		−0.0248								0.111
		(0.108)								(0.157)
Herf. Index Gov.		0.123								0.0916
		(0.0970)								(0.120)
Agg. Govern. Ind.			0.00695***							0.0107***
			(0.00245)							(0.00343)
Civil liberties				0.0749***						0.0467
				(0.0276)						(0.0304)
KOF Index of Glob.					0.0114***					0.00830
					(0.00317)					(0.00805)
Monetary freedom						0.00275				−0.000998
						(0.00246)				(0.00179)
Fiscal freedom						−0.00624				−0.000795
						(0.00414)				(0.00353)
Investment freedom							0.00142			0.000396
							(0.00176)			(0.00112)
Property rights								0.00680***		−0.00333
								(0.00192)		(0.00217)

(continued)

Table 2.2 (continued)

Variables	(1)	(2)	(3)	(4)	(5)	(6)	(7)	(8)	(9)	(10)
Log Real GDP									0.145***	−0.166
									(0.0392)	(0.121)
Constant	0.982**	0.482	0.958***	0.630**	0.825***	3.277***	0.796**	0.865***	0.611***	3.552***
	(0.448)	(0.379)	(0.332)	(0.320)	(0.200)	(0.580)	(0.372)	(0.229)	(0.213)	(0.708)
Observations	738	654	719	792	791	719	719	719	787	547
Number of countries	89	84	96	96	95	94	94	94	96	82
Hansen OIR test	0.396	0.515	0.998	0.198	1.000	1.000	0.482	1.000	1.000	1.000
AR(1)	1.99e-08	5.46e-07	4.09e-08	5.51e-09	3.47e-09	6.09e-06	8.59e-08	2.44e-08	1.83e-09	1.42e-05
AR(2)	0.301	0.909	0.251	0.230	0.206	0.300	0.314	0.375	0.201	0.616
AR(3)	0.802	0.652	0.818	0.706	0.550	0.954	0.727	0.816	0.474	0.0679

Note: Models (indicated by columns) estimated by System-GMM approach; in the parenthesis are robust standard errors ***$p < 0.01$, **$p < 0.05$, *$p < 0.1$. Models taken separately to see impact of variables individually (along with avoiding collinearity issue among variables); last model includes all the variables and checks their impact taken together. The null hypothesis of instrument set being valid exogenous is checked by the p-values of the Hansen Over-Identifying Restrictions (OIR) test. Arellano-Bond AR(1), AR(2) and AR(3) tests are used to check the null of no autocorrelation. To save space, time dummies not reported. Furthermore, all available lagged values of endogenous variables are used as instruments

Table 2.3 Dependent variable -Polity II- programme countries

Variables	(1)	(2)	(3)	(4)	(5)	(6)	(7)	(8)	(9)	(10)
Lag Polity II	0.710***	0.865***	−0.00518	0.686***	0.674***	0.605***	0.566***	0.781***	0.921***	0.864***
	(0.0502)	(0.0431)	(0.0592)	(0.0315)	(0.0471)	(0.0579)	(0.0550)	(0.0338)	(0.0150)	(0.0437)
Regime	1.340***									0.0651
	(0.340)									(0.197)
Military	−0.522*									−0.152
	(0.285)									(0.173)
Herf. Index Opp.		0.748								0.00680
		(0.473)								(0.277)
Herf. Index Gov.		0.347								0.0472
		(0.528)								(0.327)
Agg. Govern. Ind.			0.0817**							−0.0135
			(0.0395)							(0.0105)
Civil liberties				1.108***						0.530***
				(0.143)						(0.204)
KOF Index of Glob.					0.0724***					0.00736
					(0.0123)					(0.00859)
Monetary freedom						0.0273**				0.00188
						(0.0116)				(0.00943)
Fiscal freedom						−0.0172				−0.00219
						(0.0185)				(0.00876)
Investment freedom							0.0621***			0.000173
							(0.0110)			(0.00602)
Property Rights								0.0246**		−0.00454
								(0.0115)		(0.00739)

(continued)

Table 2.3 (continued)

Variables	(1)	(2)	(3)	(4)	(5)	(6)	(7)	(8)	(9)	(10)
Log Real GDP									0.0917	0.0552
									(0.0600)	(0.104)
Constant	−1.082***	0.716	−0.115	−4.577***	−3.628***	0.908	−1.127**	−0.0203	−0.961*	−1.465
	(0.317)	(0.743)	(1.415)	(0.560)	(0.571)	(1.764)	(0.507)	(0.445)	(0.498)	(1.023)
Observations	2722	1841	1179	2892	2845	1444	1444	1444	2721	902
Number of cno	104	99	111	112	110	108	108	108	110	98
Hansen OIR test	1.000	1.000	1.000	1.000	1.000	1.000	1.000	1.000	1.000	1.000
AR(1)	8.66e-11	8.02e-06	0.263	1.26e-10	0	1.22e-06	8.80e-06	1.40e-05	1.34e-10	0.0784
AR(2)	0.674	0.279	0.135	0.854	0.827	0.233	0.318	0.316	0.599	0.181
AR(3)	0.169	0.690	0.805	0.186	0.181	0.415	0.491	0.452	0.275	0.425

Note: Models (indicated by columns) estimated by System-GMM approach; in the parenthesis are robust standard errors ***$p < 0.01$, **$p < 0.05$, *$p < 0.1$. Models taken separately to see impact of variables individually (along with avoiding collinearity issue among variables); last model includes all the variables and checks their impact taken together. The null hypothesis of instrument set being valid exogenous is checked by the p-values of the Hansen Over-Identifying Restrictions (OIR) test. Arellano-Bond AR(1), AR(2) and AR(3) tests are used to check the null of no autocorrelation. To save space, time dummies not reported. Furthermore, all available lagged values of endogenous variables are used as instruments

Table 2.4 Dependent variable -EFI- prolonged users

Variables	(1)	(2)	(3)	(4)	(5)	(6)	(7)	(8)	(9)	(10)
Lag EFI	0.704***	0.721***	0.391***	0.666***	0.886***	0.564***	0.0228	0.0747	0.735***	0.500***
	(0.0672)	(0.0496)	(0.0809)	(0.0450)	(0.0297)	(0.0673)	(0.0828)	(0.0681)	(0.0520)	(0.0578)
Regime	0.149**									0.275
	(0.0633)									(0.230)
Military	−0.193**									−0.414**
	(0.0925)									(0.195)
Herf. Index Opp.		0.0487								0.177
		(0.110)								(0.126)
Herf. Index Gov.		0.219								0.162
		(0.136)								(0.159)
Agg. Govern. Ind.			0.0154***							0.0108**
			(0.00493)							(0.00443)
Civil liberties				0.0904**						−0.0419
				(0.0402)						(0.0426)
KOF Index of Glob.					0.00363*					−0.00171
					(0.00214)					(0.00598)
Monetary freedom						0.00131				−0.00167
						(0.00277)				(0.00313)
Fiscal freedom						0.00465				0.00204
						(0.00531)				(0.00346)
Investment freedom							0.000752			−0.000238
							(0.00238)			(0.00178)
Property rights								0.00188		−0.00515
								(0.00393)		(0.00315)

(continued)

Table 2.4 (continued)

Variables	(1)	(2)	(3)	(4)	(5)	(6)	(7)	(8)	(9)	(10)
Log Real GDP									0.130*	−0.0905
									(0.0712)	(0.180)
Constant	1.821***	1.631***	3.315***	1.828***	0.523***	2.221***	5.870***	5.973***	0.856**	3.665***
	(0.406)	(0.364)	(0.499)	(0.314)	(0.145)	(0.559)	(0.541)	(0.485)	(0.384)	(1.064)
Observations	297	283	272	301	301	293	293	293	298	251
Number of countries	36	36	37	37	37	37	37	37	37	36
Hansen OIR test	1.000	1.000	1.000	1.000	1.000	1.000	1.000	1.000	1.000	1.000
AR(1)	0.000401	9.75e-05	0.000212	5.23e-05	6.17e-05	0.000112	0.544	0.205	2.64e-05	0.000265
AR(2)	0.0954	0.200	0.0177	0.0997	0.0910	0.0870	0.163	0.141	0.103	0.130
AR(3)	0.177	0.165	0.286	0.143	0.183	0.108	0.316	0.259	0.203	0.576

Note: Models (indicated by columns) estimated by System-GMM approach; in the parenthesis are robust standard errors ***$p < 0.01$, **$p < 0.05$, *$p<0.1$. Models taken separately to see impact of variables individually (along with avoiding collinearity issue among variables); last model includes all the variables and checks their impact taken together. The null hypothesis of instrument set being valid exogenous is checked by the p-values of the Hansen Over-Identifying Restrictions (OIR) test. Arellano-Bond AR(1), AR(2) and AR(3) tests are used to check the null of no autocorrelation. To save space, time dummies not reported. Furthermore, all available lagged values of endogenous variables are used as instruments

Table 2.5 Dependent variable -Polity II- prolonged users

Variables	(1)	(2)	(3)	(4)	(5)	(6)	(7)	(8)	(9)	(10)
Lag Polity II	0.634***	0.763***	0.674***	0.645***	0.577***	0.648***	0.388***	0.594***	0.907***	0.895***
	(0.0658)	(0.0501)	(0.138)	(0.0453)	(0.0626)	(0.0906)	(0.0808)	(0.0940)	(0.0163)	(0.0413)
Regime	0.938*									0.276
	(0.532)									(0.229)
Military	−1.000**									0.0619
	(0.444)									(0.272)
Herf. Index Opp.		−0.0950								−0.388
		(0.375)								(0.511)
Herf. Index Gov.		0.463								0.120
		(0.717)								(0.562)
Agg. Govern. Ind.			0.0159							−0.00721
			(0.0355)							(0.00938)
Civil liberties				0.965***						0.312*
				(0.149)						(0.165)
KOF Index of Glob.					0.0913***					0.0169*
					(0.0231)					(0.00942)
Monetary freedom						0.0228**				0.00392
						(0.0109)				(0.00869)
Fiscal freedom						0.0523				0.00764
						(0.0343)				(0.00827)
Investment freedom							0.0562***			−0.00405
							(0.0169)			(0.00594)
Property rights								0.0415*		−0.00242
								(0.0226)		(0.00907)

(continued)

Table 2.5 (continued)

Variables	(1)	(2)	(3)	(4)	(5)	(6)	(7)	(8)	(9)	(10)
Log Real GDP									0.248***	0.00336
									(0.0694)	(0.0964)
Constant	1.293**	0.0274	0.560	−4.771***	−3.211***	−4.601	−1.060	−0.883	−2.565***	−2.459*
	(0.515)	(0.812)	(1.209)	(0.720)	(1.050)	(3.262)	(1.104)	(1.266)	(0.739)	(1.334)
Observations	1142	730	465	1154	1154	597	597	597	1135	403
Number of countries	42	42	43	43	43	43	43	43	43	42
Hansen OIR test	1.000	1.000	1.000	1.000	1.000	1.000	1.000	0.920	1.000	1.000
AR(1)	1.03e-05	0.000795	0.112	2.38e-05	2.27e-05	0.00911	0.00265	0.0111	9.03e-06	0.122
AR(2)	0.589	0.414	0.686	0.409	0.472	0.300	0.333	0.233	0.727	0.134
AR(3)	0.314	0.315	0.578	0.520	0.388	0.354	0.387	0.351	0.417	0.859

Note: Models (indicated by columns) estimated by System-GMM approach; in the parenthesis are robust standard errors ***$p < 0.01$, **$p < 0.05$, *$p < 0.1$. Models taken separately to see impact of variables individually (along with avoiding collinearity issue among variables); last model includes all the variables and checks their impact taken together. The null hypothesis of instrument set being valid exogenous is checked by the p-values of the Hansen Over-Identifying Restrictions (OIR) test. Arellano-Bond AR(1), AR(2) and AR(3) tests are used to check the null of no autocorrelation. To save space, time dummies not reported. Furthermore, all available lagged values of endogenous variables are used as instruments

negatively impacts political institutional quality in the case of both programme countries and prolonged users. At the same time, in the case of economic institutional quality while the negative impact becomes insignificant in the case of programme countries, the impact remains negative and significant for prolonged users.

Both the estimated Herfindahl Index Opposition and Herfindahl Index Government point out that excessive strength of either opposition or government in parliament remained inconsequential for improving institutional quality (in the case of programme countries and prolonged users).

The estimated aggregate governance indicator indicates that improvement in the governance level has a positive consequence for economic institutional quality, in the case of programme countries and prolonged users. The same is true for political institutional quality in the case of programme countries, while the positive bearing of aggregate governance indicator becomes insignificant in the case of prolonged users. This significantly positive impact on institutional quality, underlines the importance of state in providing the right kind of environment for the market to function properly (Toye 1993), which includes reducing the underlying transaction costs involved in the economic activity (a result emphasized by NIE).

It is important to have civil liberties, as its estimated results for both programme countries and prolonged users hold a significantly positive bearing on institutional quality.

Level of openness, which is captured by the KOF index of globalization, comes out to be a key player in improving overall institutional quality, since it is significantly positive in the case of programme countries, as well as prolonged users.

Among other variables, monetary freedom and investment freedom are estimated to remain consequential for political institutional quality, since they have significantly positive bearing in the case of programme countries and prolonged users. The same positive impact becomes insignificant in the case of economic institutional quality. Moreover, estimated fiscal freedom does not significantly impact institutional quality.

The importance of property rights is paramount in the literature of NIE. Acemoglu and Robinson (2012) for example, pointed out that the reason why countries like United Kingdom (UK) and the Netherlands developed far quicker than its other neighbours is because of the protection of property rights that led to greater research, and innovation. The current study estimates that property rights significantly and positively impact PIQ, in the case of both programme countries and prolonged users. Furthermore, while the impact remains significantly positive for economic institutional quality in the case of programme countries, the positive impact becomes insignificant in the case of prolonged users (may be due to the absence of complementing institutional framework, like rule of law that efficiently enforces property rights to the extent that they significantly enhance EIQ).

Economic institutional quality, in the case of programme countries and prolonged users, is impacted positively and significantly by real economic growth. At the same time, impact on political institutional quality becomes insignificant in the case of programme countries. Having said that, the estimated impact of real economic growth on political institutional quality comes out to be significant and positive in the case of prolonged users.

It may be noted here, that all variables discussed above are estimated in one model (model/column [10]). It can be seen here that many of the variables lose their significance when taken together. Having said that, aggregate governance indicator, civil liberties, and KOF index of globalization remain positive and significant in terms of their impact for overall institutional quality; while military in power significantly reduces it. It may be that other determinants, although are significant individually, but in the absence of strong overall institutional quality of supporting institutional setup, they lose their significance when taken together. Hence, it is important that impact of institutional determinants is made stronger through enhanced focus on them and their supporting institutional environment.

2.4.1 *Robustness Check*

The robustness check is to compare the programme countries results (Tables 2.2 and 2.3) with the overall member countries (Tables 2.6 and 2.7), respectively for both EIQ and PIQ. Most of the results are the same in both the programme- and overall member countries for the economic- and political institutional quality models, respectively. This shows that our results are robust for all countries.

2.5 Conclusion

The current study is an attempt to determine the variables that significantly impact both the economic- and political institutional quality in the IMF programme countries. While the results brought forth in the concluding remarks pertain to programme countries, the current study also looks at the special case of prolonged users. The panel data for the above groups of countries has been analysed for the period 1980–2009, which coincides with a time of active involvement of IMF with its member countries, in terms of both technical and financial support. Furthermore, the analysis has been carried out using a System-GMM approach.

The results show that the dynamic process is highly persistent for both economic- and political institutional quality, highlighting the aspect of path dependent nature of evolution of institutional quality. As per estimations, a parliamentary form of government, aggregate governance indicator, civil liberties, level of openness, and property rights are conducive for enhancing overall institutional quality. Moreover, greater monetary- and investment freedom contribute positively to political institutional quality; while economic growth holds a positive consequence for economic institutional quality. On the other hand, military in power impacts negatively on political institutional quality.

Appendix

Table 2.6 Dependent variable -EFI- all member countries

Variables	(1)	(2)	(3)	(4)	(5)	(6)	(7)	(8)	(9)	(10)
Lag EFI	0.677***	0.965***	0.626***	0.806***	0.779***	0.850***	0.847***	0.820***	0.763***	0.525***
	(0.0434)	(0.0320)	(0.0577)	(0.0470)	(0.0361)	(0.0339)	(0.0347)	(0.0262)	(0.0390)	(0.0332)
Regime	0.380***									0.166
	(0.0885)									(0.123)
Military	−0.0930									0.0337
	(0.146)									(0.150)
Herf. Index Opp.		−0.00228								0.122
		(0.0283)								(0.114)
Herf. Index Gov.		0.0311								0.121
		(0.0271)								(0.0869)
Agg. Govern. Ind.			0.0109**							0.00802**
			(0.00533)							(0.00318)
Civil liberties				0.0758***						0.0475*
				(0.0195)						(0.0258)
KOF Index of Glob.					0.00585***					0.0162**
					(0.00226)					(0.00657)
Monetary freedom						0.00413				−0.000757
						(0.00299)				(0.00153)
Fiscal freedom						0.00138				−0.000313
						(0.00222)				(0.00284)
Investment freedom							0.00125			−0.00123
							(0.00152)			(0.00102)
Property rights								0.00552***		−0.00132
								(0.00113)		(0.00188)

(continued)

Table 2.6 (continued)

Variables	(1)	(2)	(3)	(4)	(5)	(6)	(7)	(8)	(9)	(10)
Log Real GDP									0.0562**	−0.176
									(0.0236)	(0.123)
Constant	2.055***	0.141	2.018***	0.959***	1.168***	0.621**	0.988***	0.984***	1.158***	3.041***
	(0.275)	(0.222)	(0.418)	(0.278)	(0.180)	(0.245)	(0.198)	(0.159)	(0.206)	(0.654)
Observations	1071	933	1051	1164	1146	1056	1056	1056	1150	796
Number of countries	126	117	139	139	135	135	135	135	138	115
Hansen OIR test	0.119	0.326	0.317	0.0985	1.000	1.000	0.980	0.999	1.000	1.000
AR(1)	8.66e-09	1.87e-08	2.24e-08	7.26e-10	1.06e-10	7.84e-10	3.21e-09	1.17e-10	9.84e-10	1.46e-07
AR(2)	0.0902	0.590	0.0921	0.0677	0.0645	0.0926	0.100	0.125	0.0561	0.801
AR(3)	0.349	0.579	0.590	0.252	0.202	0.220	0.261	0.330	0.121	0.760

Note: Models (indicated by columns) estimated by System-GMM approach; in the parenthesis are robust standard errors ***$p < 0.01$, **$p < 0.05$, *$p < 0.1$. Models taken separately to see impact of variables individually (along with avoiding collinearity issue among variables); last model includes all the variables and checks their impact taken together. The null hypothesis of instrument set being valid exogenous is checked by the p-values of the Hansen Over-Identifying Restrictions (OIR) test. Arellano-Bond AR(1), AR(2) and AR(3) tests are used to check the null of no autocorrelation. To save space, time dummies not reported. Furthermore, all available lagged values of endogenous variables are used as instruments

Table 2.7 Dependent variable -Polity II- all member countries

Variables	(1)	(2)	(3)	(4)	(5)	(6)	(7)	(8)	(9)	(10)
Lag Polity II	0.785***	0.828***	0.0459	0.714***	0.746***	0.690***	0.603***	0.798***	0.938***	0.723***
	(0.0428)	(0.0423)	(0.0558)	(0.0292)	(0.0463)	(0.0558)	(0.0536)	(0.0396)	(0.0123)	(0.0756)
Regime	1.449***									0.464
	(0.357)									(0.594)
Military	–0.254									−0.0862
	(0.240)									(0.688)
Herf. Index Opp.		0.169								−0.189
		(0.209)								(0.350)
Herf. Index Gov.		−0.501								−0.710
		(0.307)								(0.465)
Agg. Govern. Ind.			0.0434							0.0142
			(0.0295)							(0.0140)
Civil liberties				1.093***						0.684***
				(0.138)						(0.259)
KOF Index of Glob.					0.0508***					−0.00653
					(0.0105)					(0.0186)
Monetary freedom						0.0256**				0.00114
						(0.0103)				(0.00869)
Fiscal freedom						−0.0251				−0.00117
						(0.0165)				(0.0116)
Investment freedom							0.0661***			−0.00736
							(0.0106)			(0.00527)
Property rights								0.0104		0.00452
								(0.00924)		(0.00674)

(continued)

Table 2.7 (continued)

Variables	(1)	(2)	(3)	(4)	(5)	(6)	(7)	(8)	(9)	(10)
Log Real GDP									0.0447	−0.139
									(0.0439)	(0.168)
Constant	−0.674***	1.271***	0.973	−3.907***	−1.992***	1.225	−2.301***	1.358**	−0.443	−0.394
	(0.233)	(0.452)	(1.309)	(0.569)	(0.466)	(1.333)	(0.518)	(0.586)	(0.334)	(1.719)
Observations	3977	2730	1677	4154	4107	2066	2066	2069	3886	1259
Number of countries	149	134	157	158	156	154	154	154	155	133
Hansen OIR test	1.000	1.000	1.000	1.000	1.000	1.000	1.000	1.000	1.000	1.000
AR(1)	0	8.68e-06	0.116	0	0	5.34e-07	3.02e-06	1.33e-05	0	0.0412
AR(2)	0.905	0.205	0.128	0.754	0.718	0.209	0.279	0.261	0.400	0.0526
AR(3)	0.303	0.925	0.200	0.333	0.319	0.455	0.536	0.482	0.532	0.343

Note: Models (indicated by columns) estimated by System-GMM approach; in the parenthesis are robust standard errors ***$p < 0.01$, **$p < 0.05$, *$p < 0.1$. Models taken separately to see impact of variables individually (along with avoiding collinearity issue among variables); last model includes all the variables and checks their impact taken together. The null hypothesis of instrument set being valid exogenous is checked by the p-values of the Hansen Over-Identifying Restrictions (OIR) test. Arellano-Bond AR(1), AR(2) and AR(3) tests are used to check the null of no autocorrelation. To save space, time dummies not reported. Furthermore, all available lagged values of endogenous variables are used as instruments

References

Abbott P, Andersen TB, Tarp F (2010) IMF and economic reform in developing countries. Q Rev Econ Finance 50:17–26
Acemoglu D (2006) A simple model of inefficient institutions. Scand J Econ 108:515–546
Acemoglu D, Johnson S (2005) Unbundling institutions. J Polit Econ 113:949–995
Acemoglu D, Robinson JA (2008) Persistence of power, elites, and institutions. Am Econ Rev 98:267–293
Acemoglu D, Robinson JA (2012) Why nations fail: the origins of power, prosperity, and poverty, 1st edn. Crown Business, New York, NY
Acemoglu D, Johnson S, Robinson J (2001a) The colonial origins of comparative development: an empirical investigation. Am Econ Rev 91:1369–1401
Acemoglu D, Johnson S, Robinson J (2001b) Reversal of fortune: geography and institutions in the making of the modern world income distribution, MIT Working paper No. 01–38. MIT Press, Cambridge
Acemoglu D, Johnson S, Robinson J, Thaicharoen Y (2003) Institutional causes, macroeconomic symptoms: volatility, crises and growth. J Monet Econ 50:49–123
Afonso A, Jalles JT (2011) Economic performance and government size. ECB Working paper series No. 1399. ECB, Germany
Ahmadov I, Mammadov J, Aslanli K (2013) Assessment of institutional quality in resource-rich Caspian Basin countries. Khazar University, Baku. http://mpra.ub.uni-muenchen.de/47430/. Accessed 10 Nov 2013
Alonso JA, Garcimartin C (2013) The determinants of institutional quality. More on the debate. J Int Dev 25:206–226
Arellano M, Bond S (1991) Some tests of specification for panel data: Monte Carlo evidence and an application to employment equations. Rev Econ Stud 58:277–297
Arellano M, Bover O (1995) Another look at instrumental variables estimation of error-component models. J Econ 68:29–51
Arpac O, Bird G, Mandilaras A (2008) Stop interrupting: an empirical analysis of the implementation of IMF programs. World Dev 36:1493–1513
Barro RJ, Lee J (2005) IMF programmes: who is chosen and what are the effects? J Monet Econ 52:1245–1269
Bird G (2001) IMF programmes: do they work? Can they be made to work better? World Dev 29:1849–1865
Bird G (2007) The IMF: a bird's eye view of its role and operations. J Econ Surv 21:683–745
Bird G, Willett T (2004) IMF conditionality, implementation and the new political economy of ownership. Comp Econ Stud 46:423–450
Blundell R, Bond S (1998) Initial conditions and moment restrictions in dynamic panel data models. J Econ 87:115–143
Buira A (1983) IMF financial programs and conditionality. J Dev Econ 12:111–136
Chavance B (2009) Institutional economics, 1st edn. Routledge, London. Originally published in French, Paris (2007)
Coase R (1992) The institutional structure of production. Am Econ Rev 82:713–719
Evrensel AY (2002) Effectiveness of IMF-supported stabilization programmes in developing countries. J Int Money Finance 21:565–587
Groenewegen J, Spithoven A, van den Berg A (2010) Institutional economics: an introduction, 1st edn. Palgrave Macmillan, Hampshire
Gwartney J, Lawson R (2003) The concept and measurement of economic freedom. Eur J Polit Econ 19:405–430
Hall RE, Jones CI (1999) Why do some countries produce so much more output per worker than others? Q J Econ 114:83–116
Hansen LP (1982) Large sample properties of generalized method of moments estimators. Econometrica 50:1029–1054

Harriss J, Hunter J, Lewis CM (1995) The new institutional economics and third world, 2nd edn. Routledge, London
IEO/IMF (2002) Report of the Independent Evaluation Office (IEO) on prolonged use of IMF resources. IMF, Washington, DC
IEO/IMF (2007) An IEO evaluation of structural conditionality in IMF-supported programs. IMF, Washington, DC
IMF (2005a) IMF conditionality. Factsheet. http://www.imf.org/external/np/exr/facts/conditio.htm. Accessed 10 Dec 2013
IMF (2005b) Building institutions. In World economic outlook, Building institutions, World economic and financial surveys. IMF, Washington, DC, pp 125–160
Javed O (2015) Institutional determinants: a case study of IMF programme and non-programme countries. In: Schofield N, Caballero G (eds) The political economy of governance: institutions, political performance and elections, 1st edn. Springer, Switzerland
Joskow PL (2008) Introduction to new institutional economics: a report card. In: Brousseau E, Glachant J-M (eds) New Institutional economics: a guidebook, 1st edn. Cambridge University Press, Cambridge, pp 1–19
Kaufmann D, Kraay A, Mastruzzi M (2010) The worldwide governance indicators: methodology and analytical issues. World Bank policy research working paper No. 5430. The World Bank, Washington, DC
Knack S, Keefer P (1997) Does social capital have an economic payoff? A cross-country investigation. Q J Econ 112:1251–1288
Kormendi RC, Meguire PG (1985) Macroeconomic determinants of growth: cross- country evidence. J Monet Econ 16:141–163
Kuncic A (2014) Institutional quality dataset. J Inst Econ 10:135–161
La Porta R, Lopez-De-Silanes F, Shleifer A, Vishny RW (1997) Legal determinants of external finance. J Finance 52:1131–1150
Marshall MG, Jaggers K, Gurr TR (2011) Polity IV project: dataset users' manual. Polity IV project, Arlington, VA
Milgrom P, North D, Weingast B (1990) The role of institutions in the revival of trade: the medieval law merchant. Econ Polit 2:1–23
North D (1990) Institutions, institutional change, and economic performance, 1st edn. Cambridge University Press, New York, NY
North D (1994) Institutional change: a framework of analysis. Washington University, St. Louis, MO. http://papers.ssrn.com/sol3/papers.cfm?abstract_id=6041. Accessed 10 Nov 2013
North DC (2005) Understanding the process of economic change (Princeton economic history of the western World), 1st edn. Princeton University Press, Princeton, NJ
Nsouli SM, Atoian R, Mourmouras A (2004) Institutions, program implementation, and macroeconomic performance. IMF working paper No. 04–184. IMF, Washington, DC
Nugent JB, Robinson JA (2002) Are endowments fate? Centre for Economic Policy Research discussion paper No. 3206. Centre for Economic Policy Research, London
Quibria MG (2002) Growth and poverty: lessons from the East Asian miracle revisited. Asian Development Bank research paper No. 33. Asian Development Bank Institute, Tokyo
Rodrik D (2000) Institutions for high-quality growth: what they are and how to acquire them. NBER Working paper No. 7540. NBER, Cambridge
Rodrik D (2005) Growth strategies. In: Philippe A, Steven D (eds) Handbook of economic growth, 1st edn. Elsevier, Philadelphia, PA, pp 1–14
Rodrik D, Subramanian A, Trebbi F (2002) Institutions rule: the primacy of institutions over geography and integration in economic development. Centre for Economic Policy Research discussion paper series No. 3643. Centre for Economic Policy Research, London
Roodman D (2007) A short note on the theme of too many instruments. Center for Global Development working papers 125. Center for Global Development, Washington, DC
Roodman D (2009) How to do xtabond2: an introduction to difference and system GMM in Stata. Stata J 9:86–136

Scully GW (1988) The institutional framework and economic development. J Polit Econ 96:652–662
Shirley MM (2008) Institutions and development. In: Menard C, Shirley MM (eds) Handbook of new institutional economics, 1st edn. Springer, New York, NY, pp 611–638
Smith A (1976) An inquiry into the nature and causes of the wealth of nations, 1st edn. Campbell RH, Skinner AS (eds) Oxford University Press, Oxford. Liberty Classics reprint, 1981. Originally published in London (1776)
Stiglitz JE (2001) Failure of the fund: rethinking the IMF response. Harv Int Rev 23:14–18
Toye J (1993) Dilemmas of development, 2nd edn. Routledge, London
Ugur M (2010) Institutions and economic performance: a review of the theory and evidence. MPRA paper 25909. University Library of Munich, Munich. http://mpra.ub.uni-muenchen.de/25909/. Accessed 10 Nov 2013
Vreeland J (2006) IMF program compliance: aggregate index versus policy specific research strategies. Rev Int Organ 1:359–378
Williamson OE (1975) Markets and hierarchies. Analysis and antitrust implications, 1st edn. Free Press, New York, NY
Williamson OE (1985) The economic institutions of capitalism, 1st edn. Free Press, New York, NY

Chapter 3
Institutional Quality, Macroeconomic Stabilization and Economic Growth: A Case Study of IMF Programme Countries

Abstract In this chapter the impact of the significant institutional determinants (obtained from Chap. 2) is then estimated on real economic growth, both directly, and also indirectly, through the channel of macroeconomic stability. Results mainly validate that institutional determinants overall play a positive role in reducing macroeconomic instability, and through it, and also independently, enhance real economic growth.

3.1 Introduction[1]

During the last three decades or so, many countries have received once or have been prolonged users of IMF resources, but research literature points to the fact that most of them have not been able to achieve macroeconomic stability on a sustained basis (Evrensel 2002; Easterly 2005).

Article IV, Section 1 of IMF's Article of Agreement,[2] identifies one of the essential roles of IMF as a facilitator of member countries in reaching the objective of sustained economic growth. Notwithstanding the criticism of IMF programmes in terms of their Neo-Classical/Monetarist basis, Enhanced Structural Adjustment Facility (ESAF; established in 1987)[3] of the Fund for low-income countries, practically underlined the shifting focus of IMF from the surveillance and BOP to both the BOP and growth objective. But, a programme basis well entrenched in orthodox economic thought, meant lack of any attempt by IMF to adopt more heterodox thought process, for example in the shape of NIE, appears to have been a

[1] There are two earlier versions of this paper. One can be found at 'Munich Personal RePEc Archive' (http://mpra.ub.uni-muenchen.de/). It was place there on 6th June, 2014 (https://mpra.ub.uni-muenchen.de/secure/cgi/users/home?screen=EPrint%3A%3AView&eprintid=56370); while the other has been placed as a UB Economics [Faculty of Economics and Business, University of Barcelona (UB)] working paper (http://www.ub.edu/ubeconomics/wp-content/uploads/2013/07/Paper-2_Omer-Javed.pdf).

[2] http://www.imf.org/external/pubs/ft/aa/pdf/aa.pdf

[3] ESAF later in 1999 was renamed as, 'Poverty Reduction and Growth Facility' (PRGF; http://www.imf.org/external/np/exr/chron/chron.asp).

O. Javed, *The Economic Impact of International Monetary Fund Programmes*, Contributions to Economics, DOI 10.1007/978-3-319-29178-9_3

major cause for the non-performance of IMF programmes in terms of economic growth consequences for programme countries (especially the prolonged users). Hence, it has been pointed out that too much focus of the IMF on the demand side of the economy, at the cost of supply side, has led to the impact of IMF programmes at most being neutral (and in some countries even negative) on economic growth of programme countries (Haque and Khan 1998; Bird 2001, 2007; Arpac et al. 2008).

NIE literature, on the other hand, indicates that countries which saw improvement in institutional quality, also witnessed their income per capita improving (Acemoglu and Johnson 2005; Afonso and Jalles 2011). Actually, NIE points out that by focusing on improving determinants of institutional quality (for example, by reducing transaction costs, by protecting property rights, by ensuring enforcement of contracts, and by improving rule of law, etc.) the overall institutional environment improves, and has a positive impact on both the macroeconomic situation and economic growth.

Given the consequence of IMF programmes at most being neutral for economic growth, on one hand, and institutional determinants significantly and positively affecting economic growth in countries overall, on the other hand, the paper intends to explore the possibility that significant institutional determinants (obtained from Chap. 2) may positively impact real GDP both directly, and then indirectly through the macroeconomic stability channel, in IMF programme countries.

The study is structured in the following way: relevant literature is reviewed in Sect. 3.2, followed by discussion of data and methodology in Sect. 3.3, while Sect. 3.4 highlights estimation and results. Conclusion of the study is given in the last section (which is Sect. 3.5).

3.2 Literature Review

Ever since the Third World Debt crisis of the 1980s, IMF enhanced its role, mainly through its structural adjustment window; resulting in turn, in greater focus of economic research to gauge the impact of IMF programmes on the economic performance of recipient countries.

A lot of countries have been under the IMF programmes during the last three decades. Therefore, there has been an effort by researchers to understand the impact of these programmes, for which different approaches have been employed. Haque and Khan (1998, p. 7) pointed out that the difference between these methodologies fundamentally lay in the way the ‘counterfactual’ was formulated, which served as a benchmark to gauge the performance of the ‘actual outcome’ against a macroeconomic outcome existing in a world of no programme (i.e., the ‘counterfactual’).

Haque and Khan (1998, pp. 8–12) indicated that due to informational constraints with regard to structural parameters and policy reaction function parameters, different programme evaluation methods construct counterfactuals differently; with approaches being (i) before-after (BA; evaluates macroeconomic performance under and before the programme; but suffers from over-simplification by excluding the impact of any exogenous factors), (ii) with-without (WW; where a group of non-programme countries is taken as a 'control group' and the performance of a programme country is compared with it; with major shortcoming in terms of assuming that programme and non-programme countries are same prior to the start of the programme, which is especially problematic given the programme country is crisis hit to start with, suffering in turn the non-random selection bias with regard to selection of programme countries), (iii) generalized evaluation estimator (GEE) approach (while it also compares programme and non-programme countries, it controls for initial conditions and exogenous influences), and (iv) comparison of simulations (SIM; compares simulated performance of countries under hypothetical Fund programmes and non-Fund policies; but has the shortcoming that the required underlying econometric model that captured the whole spectrum of a typical Fund programme, is not available).

Using BA approach, while Khan and Knight (1981) reported a negative impact, Killick et al. (1992) pointed towards a positive impact of IMF programmes on economic growth of recipient countries; where Evrensel (2002) indicated a neutral impact on economic growth. Similarly, using WW approach, while Donovan (1981) found out a positive impact of Fund programmes on economic growth, Loxley (1984) pointed towards a neutral effect on growth. Hence, the underlying weak assumptions with regard to formulation of counterfactual in the BA and WW approaches may be the reason why different studies using these methodologies produced results that are all over the place, making it difficult to conclude anything substantively with regard to the impact of IMF programmes on economic growth of recipient countries.

Having said that, formulation of a more informed counterfactual, using GEE methodology gave more consistent results, which more often than not indicated that Fund programmes had a negative impact on economic growth of recipient countries. Hence, for example, Goldstein and Montiel (1986) using data from 1974 to 1981, and employing GEE methodology pointed out a negative impact of Fund programmes on economic growth. Similarly, Barro and Lee (2005) using GEE methodology (and by employing data from 1975 to 2000) indicated that Fund lending retarded economic growth. Also, Dreher (2006), who covered a time period from 1970 to 2000, pointed out an overall negative impact on economic growth. Furthermore, Nsouli et al. (2004) also indicated that Fund programmes remained neutral in terms of their impact on economic growth.

A further review of literature to see the detailed impact of IMF programmes revealed a poor performance in terms of individual macroeconomic indicators of recipient countries, along with highlighting the emergence and persistence of recidivism in IMF programme countries. While Khan (1990) and Pastor (1987) discovered significant positive impacts on the overall balance of payments, Conway (2006) indicated that the impact had reduced since the 1970s and 1980s. Evrensel (2002, p. 586) found out that previous programme countries entered a new one at the back of an even worse macroeconomic situation (as compared to the situation when they were not in the programme in the first place), because of the existence of moral hazard in terms of easily available financing. Also, he indicated that significant improvement achieved in terms of current account and foreign exchange reserves, could not be sustained after the programme ended. Similarly, Przeworski and Vreeland (2000), using data from 1951 to 1990, showed that countries in a programme saw their growth rates decreasing; whereas the same countries otherwise grew faster once they left the programme.

Moreover, research conducted by Barro and Lee (2005) did not see any significant consequence of IMF programmes for either investment or inflation; and could not find positive consequence on economic growth in recipient countries, which remained frequent borrowers from IMF. Bird (1996) pointed out that till the time Fund programmes put improving economic growth as the top priority on its agenda, recipient countries would continue to remain recidivist. Similar consequence was highlighted by Hutchison and Noy (2003) while gauging the impact of Fund programmes in Latin American, pointed out low programme completion rates and recidivism, high output costs, and no improvement in current account.

Butkiewicz and Yanikkaya (2005) using actual monetary values of IMF lending (rather than the number of programmes approved by the Fund, since according to the them there remained a high level of non-completion of IMF programmes) pointed out that while Fund's overall objective for crisis-hit countries was to put them on stable economic growth footings, yet the impact of Fund programmes in this regard, was either neutral or negative, given their policies had an adverse impact for public and private investment; revealing in turn that the Fund in putting too much emphasis on the demand side, neglected the supply side of the economy in the process. One of the main steps in this regard according to NIE, is improving institutions so that the transaction costs can be lowered to induce investment (which in turn helps boost economic growth).

With regard to the prolonged users, Easterly (2005) indicated that during 1980–1999 these countries were unable to achieve either reasonable growth or deal convincingly with macroeconomic distortions.

Given this background, while the Fund also realized and internalized this performance and criticism (IMF 2005; IEO 2007), researchers have criticized and asked IMF to improve its Financial Programming and Policies (FPP) framework for better results for recipient countries in terms of consequences for macroeconomic stability and economic growth (IEO 2007; Bird and Willett 2004). For instance, Bird (2007) found the criticism to be legitimate since it found IMF programmes to be 'over simplistic'. Moreover, Buira (1983) called on the Fund to revisit its financial programming techniques for certain cases. Also, Bird (2001) asked IMF to redesign its programmes. More specifically, Abbott et al. (2010) while analyzing impact of programmes on developing countries, criticized Fund to be too rigid and conventional/uniform in its approach in terms of its conditionalities, and this formed as one of the reasons for its impact neutral performance with regard to economic growth; in turn asked for a fresh approach.

In terms of suggesting specific remedies, Khan and Knight (1985), for instance, indicated the negative impact on economic growth could be restricted to short-term, in case supply-side policies were pursued. Moreover, Arpac et al. (2008) suggested to IMF to focus on domestic politics also, while forming expectations about the extent of programme implementation in a country. At the same time, Nsouli et al. (2004) pointed out that most research on gauging impact of Fund programmes did not take into account the underlying role of institutional quality in programme success rate. Furthermore, pointed out that in programme countries, better institutional quality and healthier political environment had positive consequences for macroeconomic outcomes, and programme implementation rates.

Research literature of NIE has found that improvement in institutional determinants had an overall positive and significant bearing on the economic growth of countries (for example, Rodrik et al. 2002; Hall and Jones 1999). For instance, Acemoglu et al. (2004) while analyzing the different institutions of North and South Korea, pointed out that unlike the North, in the South, political and economic institutions were strengthened for example by policy decisions that were taken democratically, and which protected private property, and developed markets. This led to greater economic growth and development in South Korea over the years, as compared to North Korea, even though both countries shared the same culture since they were one country under the Japanese occupation (which ended in 1945, and the division subsequently). Similarly, improvement in institutions (both political and economic) led Botswana experience very high growth rates during the last three decades or so (Acemoglu et al. 2003a; Parsons and Robinson 2006).

3.3 Data and Methodology

3.3.1 *Theoretical Design*

The main motivation of the current study is based on the 'missing link', which identifies itself as the effect of institutions on economic growth of IMF programme countries; given the background of a poor performance of IMF programmes for recipient countries in terms of economic growth consequence (mainly due to insufficient focus on the supply side of the economy) and the importance of institutions in improving economic growth rates in countries, as revealed by the research literature of NIE. Hence, the current study makes an effort to explore this 'missing link' by analysing the impact of institutional determinants on economic growth of IMF programme countries, with the underlying premise that improvement in institutional determinants both directly, and indirectly (through the channel of macroeconomic stability) positively impact real GDP.

As indicated earlier, NIE literature indicates that enhancement in the quality of institutions has a significantly positive bearing on real economic growth (Rodrik et al. 2002; Ugur 2010). In the current analysis, the same is being premised for IMF programme countries:

$$\text{Real GDP} = \text{f (institutional determinants, other variables)} \quad [a] \quad (+)$$

At the same time, it has been advocated, for example by Acemoglu et al. (2003b) that the main reason behind macroeconomic instability (MI) and the varying levels of macroeconomic volatility among different countries were related more with institutional reasons than the traditionally identified macroeconomic determinants. Similarly, better budgetary institutions (which are important economic institutions) had a negatively significant impact on (budget) deficit (von Hagen 1991). Hence, the current study considers the notion that improvement in institutional determinants in IMF programme countries negatively impact MI:

$$\text{MI} = \text{f(institutional determinants, other variables)} \quad [b] \quad (-)$$

In a case study of Iran conducted by Haghighi et al. (2012) it was pointed out that there existed a long-term relation between economic growth and macroeconomic instability. Therefore, lastly, it is also premised here that macroeconomic instability has a negative bearing on real GDP in IMF programme countries:

$$\text{Real GDP} = \text{f(MI, other variables)} \quad [c] \quad (-)$$

For the purpose of analysis, the institutional determinants to be employed will be the significant determinants of institutional quality obtained from Chap. 2.

3.3.2 *Sample*

Out of the total IMF member countries at 188, countries that have remained under IMF programme(s) at one time or the other (otherwise called 'programme countries') have been found out to stand at 129 during the sample period (1980–2009). Furthermore, for the purposes of analysis, programme countries have been sub-divided into two groups of 'prolonged users' and 'non-prolonged users.[4] They stand at 44 and 85, respectively, during the time period taken. At the same time, for the purpose of drawing lessons from countries that have never been under an IMF programme during 1980–2009, non-programme countries have also been taken; which stand at 59.[5]

[4] The author has used the terminology of non-prolonged users to represent a group of programme countries that have remained under an IMF programme for less than 7 years in a decade.

[5] See Table 3.11 for group-wise list of IMF member countries during 1980–2009.

3.3.3 Data and Variable Description

Data on real GDP is taken from the World Economic Outlook (WEO) of the IMF.[6]

Based on the methodology and definitions of Ismihan (2003), Macroeconomic Instability Index (MII)[7] has been constructed using the following five[8] indicators:

1. Inflation rate (INF; calculated by taking data on average consumer prices from WEO),
2. Budget deficit as percentage of GDP (BD; taken from WEO),
3. General government gross debt as percentage of GDP (GGGD; obtained from WEO),
4. Exchange rate variability (ERV) has been calculated on the basis of 12 month end-of-period nominal exchange rate in SDR (Special Drawing Rights),[9] taken from International Financial Statistics (IFS; IMF)[10] and,
5. Real Effective Exchange Rate Index (REER; taken from WDI[11] of the World Bank). This indicator has been included in Ismihan (2003) to augment MII to include the impact of competitiveness in it. Furthermore, it needs to be indicated that there exists another index in this regard called the Macroeconomic Stability Subindex,[12] produced by World Economic Forum. The reason it has not been employed in the current analysis is because of lack of consistency of its methodology; in turn, inhibiting comparability of data over longer periods of time.

Political/Governance Indicators From Chap. 2, significant variables include regime (is a dummy variable indicating 0 for presidential, and 1 for parliamentary form of government), military (chief executive a military officer or not; existence of it is represented by 1, 0 otherwise), civil liberties (data on civil liberties is taken from Freedom in the World (publication of Freedom House)[13]; where, the least rating of degree of freedom is indicated by 1, while the highest rating is represented by 7), and aggregate governance indicator (a simple average of the five indicators taken from Worldwide Governance Indicators (WGI; World Bank),[14] produced by Kaufmann et al. (2010)[15]; where these five indicators cover aspects with regard to

[6] http://www.imf.org/external/pubs/ft/weo/2011/01/weodata/download.aspx

[7] For details, see Ismihan (2003, pp. 214–215), who constructed MII.

[8] It may be indicated here that while Ismihan (2003) only included the first four indicators to construct the MII, the current study augments it with one more indicator.

[9] http://www.imf.org/external/np/exr/facts/sdr.htm

[10] Data taken from IFS CD ROM (IMF).

[11] http://data.worldbank.org/data-catalog/world-development-indicator

[12] http://www.weforum.org/pdf/Global_Competitiveness_Reports/Reports/GCR_05_06/Composition_of_the_Growth_Competitiveness_Index

[13] http://www.freedomhouse.org/report-types/freedom-world

[14] http://data.worldbank.org/data-catalog/worldwide-governance-indicators

[15] http://info.worldbank.org/governance/wgi/index.aspx#home

the level of voice and accountability, effectiveness of government, the situation of rule of law, the quality of regulations, and the extent of control of corruption).

Economic Variables From Chap. 2 significant variables include KOF Index of Globalization[16] (a proxy of openness), three measures of economic freedom and prosperity and are monetary freedom, investment freedom, and property rights (taken from the Index of Economic Freedom[17]). The other significant determinant of institutional quality from Chap. 2 is real GDP, which has not been included here, since the dependent variable is also real GDP.

Control Variables They include government spending and population taken from WDI.

Endogeneity Based on literature review (for instance discussion of institutions in NIE literature; see for example Acemoglu et al. 2001), it has been realized that the problem of endogeneity exists for many variables. In the current study, variables that may be affected by endogeneity issue include MII, government spending, aggregate governance indicator, KOF Index of Globalization, monetary freedom, investment freedom, and property rights. It may be indicated here that as lagged dependent variable is correlated with the error term, so lagged real GDP and lagged MII may cause endogeneity problem in the regression.

3.3.4 *Econometric Methodology*

As explained in the theoretical design, the purpose here is to estimate the impact of institutional determinants (obtained from Chap. 2) both directly and then indirectly (through MII) on real GDP, in terms of the two sub-groups of programme countries, i.e. 'prolonged users' and 'non-prolonged users'. Therefore, in line with this design, the first equation will be estimated as follows:

$$\mathrm{LGDP}_{it} = \alpha_i + \alpha_1 \mathrm{LGDP}_{i,t-1} + \alpha_2 \mathrm{X}_{it} + \alpha_3 \mathrm{Z}_{it} + \alpha_4 \mathrm{M}_{it} + \omega_t + \epsilon_{it} \tag{3.1}$$

where, LGDP_{it} stands for log real GDP. α_i are the country-fixed effects. $\mathrm{LGDP}_{i,t-1}$ stands for lagged log real GDP. X_{it} is a vector of significant political/governance indicators, and Z_{it} is a vector of significant economic variables; while M_{it} is a vector of control variables. ω_t are the time specific effects. ϵ_{it} is the error term.

While Eq. (3.1) is estimated to check the direct impact of significant determinants of institutional quality on real GDP, the next two equations will together indirectly estimate this impact, as follows:

[16] http://globalization.kof.ethz.ch/

[17] http://www.heritage.org/index/explore

$$MII_{it} = \beta_i + \beta_1 MII_{i,t-1} + \beta_2 X_{it} + \beta_3 Z_{it} + \gamma_t + \eta_{it} \tag{3.2}$$

where, MII_{it} stands for Macroeconomic Instability Index, while $MII_{i,t-1}$ stands for lagged MII. β_i are the country-fixed effects, while X_{it}, Z_{it}, once again are a vector of significantly positive determinants of institutional quality from Chap. 2; γ_t are the time specific effects, and η_{it} is the error term.

and,

$$LGDP_{it} = \pi_i + \pi_1 LGDP_{i,t-1} + \pi_2 \widehat{MII}_{it} + \pi_3 M_{it} + \phi_t + \varphi_{it} \tag{3.3}$$

where, $LGDP_{it}$ stands for log real GDP. π_i are the country-fixed effects. $LGDP_{i,t-1}$ stands for lagged log real GDP. $\widehat{MII}_{it}$ stands for predicted values of MII from Eq. (3.2). M_{it} are the control variables. ϕ_t are the time specific effects, while φ_{it} is the error term.

Hence, in Eq. (3.2), the impact of significant determinants of institutional quality is investigated on MII, while in Eq. (3.3) the impact of predicted MII is explored on real GDP.

The underlying premise for employing this indirect approach is to see the importance of institutional focus for IMF programmes in improving macroeconomic stability, and also, economic growth. The basis for this here is that as institutional quality improves, it will reduce macroeconomic instability, and also as macroeconomic instability decreases it will enhance real GDP.

The above Eqs. (3.1)–(3.3) are being estimated using Arellano and Bover (1995) approach. The big advantage of this approach is that it uses the information in the equations simultaneously in level and as well as difference forms. For this purpose, we take the difference of all equations, as follows:

$$\Delta LGDP_{it} = \delta_1 \Delta LGDP_{i,t-1} + \delta_2 \Delta X_{it} + \delta_3 \Delta Z_{it} + \delta_4 \Delta M_{it} + \theta_t + \varepsilon_{it} \tag{3.4}$$

$$\Delta MII_{it} = \rho_1 \Delta MII_{i,t-1} + \rho_2 \Delta X_{it} + \rho_3 \Delta Z_{it} + \tau_t + \sigma_{it} \tag{3.5}$$

$$\Delta LGDP_{it} = \xi_1 \Delta LGDP_{i,t-1} + \xi_2 \Delta \widehat{MII}_{it} + \xi_3 \Delta M_{it} + \Omega_t + \mu_{it} \tag{3.6}$$

These equations also serve the purpose of removing any possible heterogeneity in the models above (where Δ indicates change for a variable between years t and t−1).

For the estimation of the models, like the ones above, the approach of Generalized Method of Moments (GMM) has been recommended by Arellano and Bover (1995) and Blundell and Bond (1998).[18] The GMM approach, in the estimation of these types of models, enhances efficiency through addition of more instruments to the system of equations, i.e. in level and difference. Furthermore, all available lagged values of endogenous variables are used as instruments to resolve the

[18] Like in the previous chapter, the 'xtabond2' command has been employed to estimate the above system.

problem of autocorrelation. All the above models are estimated using robust standard errors to address the problem of autocorrelation and heteroskedasticity.

3.4 Estimation and Results

All the models have been estimated separately on the two sub-groups of programme countries, being 'prolonged users' and 'non-prolonged users'. The reason behind taking these two groups is based on the inherent difference in economic environment of these two sub-groups, where the prolonged users are generally composed of very underdeveloped economies (and hence the need for entering frequent IMF programmes), while the non-prolonged users are more representative of economies that are overall more developed than the prolonged users. Moreover, estimations have also been made for the purpose of understanding the importance of significant determinants of institutional quality in programme countries, in the case of non-programme countries (that never entered an IMF programme during 1980–2009).

Tables 3.1 and 3.2 highlight the impact of institutional determinants on real GDP for prolonged and non-prolonged users, respectively. On the other hand, Tables 3.3 and 3.4, estimate the impact of institutional determinants on MII (once again for both prolonged and non-prolonged users). Thereafter, Tables 3.5 and 3.6, estimate the impact of predicted MII ($\widehat{\text{MII}}$) on real GDP (in terms of the two sub-groups of programme countries). At the same time, as an extension, Tables 3.8, 3.9 and 3.10 indicate estimations for the case of non-programme countries.

Upfront it may be pertinent to indicate that instruments were valid and exogenous,[19] since they passed the Hansen-J statistic test of Over-Identifying Restrictions (OIR; Hansen 1982).

In Tables 3.1 and 3.2, lagged real GDP is positive and significant for real GDP in the case of both prolonged users and non-prolonged users; hence, highlighting the presence of dynamic process. The same consequence can be observed in the case of non-programme countries (Table 3.8). At the same time, in both the sub-groups of program countries, population in many of the models has a significantly negative bearing on real GDP, while government spending overall has a positive consequence for real GDP. The two control variables remain insignificant for real GDP, in the case of non-programme countries.

It can be seen in Tables 3.1 and 3.2 through the estimated institutional determinant 'regime', that as compared to presidential form of democracy, parliamentary form of democracy is more conducive for enhancing real GDP. The same consequence holds for the non-programme countries (Table 3.8). At the same time, a military officer as chief executive is detrimental to improvement in real GDP (i.e. has a significantly negatively impact) for the two sub-groups of the programme

[19] Roodman (2007) provides details.

Table 3.1 Dependent variable -real GDP- prolonged users

Variables	(1)	(2)	(3)	(4)	(5)	(6)	(7)	(8)
Lag Log Real GDP	0.973***	0.804***	0.877***	0.510***	0.351***	1.005***	0.342***	0.942***
	(0.00946)	(0.0347)	(0.0226)	(0.0768)	(0.0600)	(0.00434)	(0.0660)	(0.0326)
Log population	0.000873	0.0194	−0.0979**	−0.190***	−0.187***	−0.00555**	−0.199***	0.00841
	(0.00381)	(0.0256)	(0.0464)	(0.0561)	(0.0592)	(0.00232)	(0.0605)	(0.00799)
Government spending	−0.000118	−0.000120	0.000156	3.86e-05	0.000354**	0.000375*	0.000363**	−4.76e-05
	(0.000190)	(0.000286)	(0.000237)	(0.000366)	(0.000148)	(0.000219)	(0.000150)	(0.000245)
Regime	0.0348**							0.0770**
	(0.0152)							(0.0380)
Military	−0.0280**							−0.0641**
	(0.0120)							(0.0256)
Agg. Gov. Ind.		0.00133***						−1.52e-05
		(0.000465)						(0.000779)
Civil liberties			0.00694					0.000355
			(0.00544)					(0.00741)
KOF Index of Glob.				0.00438**				0.000506
				(0.00195)				(0.00135)
Monetary freedom					0.000349**			−0.000302
					(0.000166)			(0.000365)
Investment freedom						0.000578**		4.72e-05
						(0.000258)		(0.000288)
Property rights							0.000176	−0.00129
							(0.000263)	(0.000817)
Constant	0.201***	0.977**	2.420***	6.320***	7.580***	−0.0112	7.563***	0.351**
	(0.0755)	(0.487)	(0.888)	(1.131)	(1.240)	(0.0423)	(1.254)	(0.156)
Observations	590	449	596	596	596	596	596	445

(continued)

Table 3.1 (continued)

Variables	(1)	(2)	(3)	(4)	(5)	(6)	(7)	(8)
Number of countries	42	44	44	44	44	44	44	42
Hansen OIR test	1.000	1.000	1.000	1.000	1.000	1.000	1.000	1.000
AR(1)	0.000819	0.114	0.000556	0.0208	0.375	0.000716	0.366	0.0753
AR(2)	0.137	0.104	0.137	0.781	0.603	0.211	0.345	0.0862
AR(3)	0.208	0.0892	0.402	0.597	0.122	0.283	0.0327	0.412

Note: Models (indicated by columns) estimated by System-GMM approach; in the parenthesis are robust standard errors ***$p < 0.01$, **$p < 0.05$, *$p < 0.1$. Models taken separately to see impact of variables individually (along with avoiding collinearity issue among variables); last model includes all the variables and checks their impact taken together. The null hypothesis of instrument set being valid exogenous is checked by the p-values of the Hansen Over-Identifying Restrictions (OIR) test. Arellano-Bond AR(1), AR(2) and AR(3) tests are used to check the null of no autocorrelation. To save space, time dummies not reported. Furthermore, all available lagged values of endogenous variables are used as instruments

Table 3.2 Dependent variable -real GDP- non-prolonged users

Variables	(1)	(2)	(3)	(4)	(5)	(6)	(7)	(8)
Lag Log Real GDP	0.819***	0.817***	0.965***	0.892***	0.869***	0.727***	0.732***	0.856***
	(0.0740)	(0.0383)	(0.0208)	(0.0338)	(0.0446)	(0.0822)	(0.0817)	(0.0432)
Log population	−0.0454*	−0.0291**	−0.00356	−0.0252**	−0.0946	−0.0667**	−0.0658**	−0.0205
	(0.0269)	(0.0141)	(0.00581)	(0.0122)	(0.0856)	(0.0277)	(0.0276)	(0.0138)
Government spending	−7.08e-05	0.000170	0.000154	0.000341*	0.000119	−3.98e-05	7.76e-05	−0.000286
	(0.000246)	(0.000283)	(0.000392)	(0.000205)	(0.000224)	(0.000205)	(0.000193)	(0.000341)
Regime	0.113*							−0.0220
	(0.0657)							(0.0248)
Military	−0.0619*							0.0150
	(0.0376)							(0.0398)
Agg. Gov. Ind.		0.00352***						0.00351***
		(0.000986)						(0.000850)
Civil liberties			0.0139*					0.00349
			(0.00723)					(0.00458)
KOF Index of Glob.				0.00293**				0.00272**
				(0.00120)				(0.00127)
Monetary freedom					0.000656**			0.000656
					(0.000297)			(0.000672)
Investment freedom						0.000317		8.07e-06
						(0.000486)		(0.000620)
Property rights							0.000219	0.000439
							(0.000324)	(0.000539)
Constant	2.116**	1.718***	0.248	1.054**	2.502	3.206***	3.121***	1.107**
	(0.966)	(0.459)	(0.214)	(0.422)	(1.608)	(1.018)	(0.992)	(0.435)
Observations	884	726	959	960	963	963	963	665

(continued)

Table 3.2 (continued)

Variables	(1)	(2)	(3)	(4)	(5)	(6)	(7)	(8)
Number of countries	70	77	75	77	77	77	77	69
Hansen OIR test	1.000	1.000	1.000	1.000	1.000	1.000	1.000	1.000
AR(1)	0.0214	0.0679	0.0361	0.0295	0.0312	0.0134	0.0136	0.0432
AR(2)	0.0309	0.143	0.0448	0.0510	0.0378	0.0503	0.0501	0.174
AR(3)	0.176	0.299	0.193	0.195	0.202	0.118	0.124	0.341

Note: Models (indicated by columns) estimated by System-GMM approach; in the parenthesis are robust standard errors ***$p < 0.01$, **$p < 0.05$, *$p < 0.1$. Models taken separately to see impact of variables individually (along with avoiding collinearity issue among variables); last model includes all the variables and checks their impact taken together. The null hypothesis of instrument set being valid exogenous is checked by the p-values of the Hansen Over-Identifying Restrictions (OIR) test. Arellano-Bond AR(1), AR(2) and AR(3) tests are used to check the null of no autocorrelation. To save space, time dummies not reported. Furthermore, all available lagged values of endogenous variables are used as instruments

Table 3.3 Dependent variable-MII-prolonged users

Variables	(1)	(2)	(3)	(4)	(5)	(6)	(7)	(8)
Lag MII	0.509***	0.405***	0.272***	0.514***	0.340***	0.379***	0.344***	0.512***
	(0.0410)	(0.0624)	(0.0794)	(0.0367)	(0.106)	(0.0867)	(0.0464)	(0.0462)
Regime	−0.00869							−0.0262
	(0.0250)							(0.0179)
Military	0.0414**							0.0307**
	(0.0201)							(0.0147)
Agg. Gov. Ind.		−0.00139						0.000108
		(0.00103)						(0.000924)
Civil liberties			−0.0113**					−0.00582
			(0.00555)					(0.00702)
KOF Index of Glob.				−0.00171***				−0.00129*
				(0.000524)				(0.000733)
Monetary freedom					−0.00234**			0.000719
					(0.000955)			(0.000567)
Investment freedom						−0.00251		0.000347
						(0.00200)		(0.000572)
Property rights							−0.00145	0.00121
							(0.00102)	(0.000887)
Constant	0.230***	0.439***	0.338***	0.319***	0.448***	0.387***	0.320***	0.211***
	(0.0227)	(0.138)	(0.0350)	(0.0344)	(0.0756)	(0.104)	(0.0442)	(0.0650)
Observations	1089	484	1153	1153	599	599	599	448
Number of countries	42	44	44	44	44	44	44	42
Hansen OIR test	1.000	1.000	0.765	1.000	0.960	0.969	1.000	1.000

(continued)

Table 3.3 (continued)

Variables	(1)	(2)	(3)	(4)	(5)	(6)	(7)	(8)
AR(1)	3.37e-07	8.00e-05	0.000114	1.12e-07	0.00230	8.12e-05	1.09e-05	7.76e-05
AR(2)	0.0952	0.0536	0.0288	0.0791	0.00377	0.0147	0.00505	0.0684
AR(3)	0.117	0.0157	0.127	0.0804	0.960	0.571	0.588	0.00492

Note: Models (indicated by columns) estimated by System-GMM approach; in the parenthesis are robust standard errors ***$p < 0.01$, **$p < 0.05$, *$p < 0.1$. Models taken separately to see impact of variables individually (along with avoiding collinearity issue among variables); last model includes all the variables and checks their impact taken together. The null hypothesis of instrument set being valid exogenous is checked by the p-values of the Hansen Over-Identifying Restrictions (OIR) test. Arellano-Bond AR(1), AR(2) and AR(3) tests are used to check the null of no autocorrelation. To save space, time dummies not reported. Furthermore, all available lagged values of endogenous variables are used as instruments

Table 3.4 Dependent variable -MII- non-prolonged users

Variables	(1)	(2)	(3)	(4)	(5)	(6)	(7)	(8)
Lag MII	0.585***	0.437***	0.639***	0.488***	0.513***	0.591***	0.324*	0.539***
	(0.0398)	(0.0902)	(0.0426)	(0.0328)	(0.0382)	(0.0419)	(0.170)	(0.0964)
Regime	−0.0671							0.0478
	(0.0410)							(0.0389)
Military	0.00110							0.00212
	(0.0267)							(0.0241)
Agg. Gov. Ind.		−0.000509						−0.00602
		(0.00201)						(0.00378)
Civil liberties			0.00274					0.0394
			(0.00255)					(0.0371)
KOF Index of Glob.				−0.00322*				−0.00313
				(0.00167)				(0.00580)
Monetary freedom					−0.000134			0.00198
					(0.000509)			(0.00196)
Investment freedom						0.00106**		0.00205
						(0.000512)		(0.00163)
Property rights							−7.41e-05	0.00415
							(0.00304)	(0.00283)
Constant	0.283***	0.221**	0.218***	0.458***	0.289***	0.208***	0.211	0.0198
	(0.0256)	(0.0940)	(0.0185)	(0.0961)	(0.0424)	(0.0290)	(0.197)	(0.224)
Observations	1844	917	2000	2066	996	996	996	679
Number of countries	74	84	81	82	79	79	79	70
Hansen OIR test	1.000	1.000	1.000	1.000	1.000	1.000	0.293	1.000

(continued)

Table 3.4 (continued)

Variables	(1)	(2)	(3)	(4)	(5)	(6)	(7)	(8)
AR(1)	0	0.00765	3.72e-09	0	3.00e-05	1.15e-05	0.0381	0.000249
AR(2)	0.126	0.616	0.659	0.517	0.0214	0.0214	0.00726	0.758
AR(3)	0.398	0.441	0.435	0.621	0.0502	0.0388	0.173	0.424

Note: Models (indicated by columns) estimated by System-GMM approach; in the parenthesis are robust standard errors ***$p < 0.01$, **$p < 0.05$, *$p < 0.1$. Models taken separately to see impact of variables individually (along with avoiding collinearity issue among variables); last model includes all the variables and checks their impact taken together. The null hypothesis of instrument set being valid exogenous is checked by the p-values of the Hansen Over-Identifying Restrictions (OIR) test. Arellano-Bond AR(1), AR(2) and AR(3) tests are used to check the null of no autocorrelation. To save space, time dummies not reported. Furthermore, all available lagged values of endogenous variables are used as instruments

Table 3.5 Dependent variable -real GDP- prolonged users

Variables	(1)	(2)	(3)	(4)	(5)	(6)	(7)	(8)
Lag Log Real GDP	0.997***	0.809***	0.993***	1.000***	0.983***	0.999***	1.000***	0.991***
	(0.0111)	(0.0340)	(0.0113)	(0.0103)	(0.0162)	(0.0121)	(0.0115)	(0.00981)
Log population	−0.0140***	0.0192	−0.0165***	−0.0134***	−0.0214***	−0.00320	−0.00347	−0.00173
	(0.00517)	(0.0250)	(0.00519)	(0.00468)	(0.00709)	(0.00319)	(0.00303)	(0.00380)
Government spending	−0.000134	−0.000180	−3.07e-05	−0.000206	−6.49e-05	5.19e-06	−8.58e-05	0.000106
	(0.000459)	(0.000278)	(0.000419)	(0.000407)	(0.000561)	(0.000367)	(0.000365)	(0.000377)
Predicted MII: Regime & Military	−0.0676							
	(0.0684)							
Predicted MII: Agg. Gov. Ind.		−0.104***						
		(0.0351)						
Predicted MII: Civil liberties			−0.0766					
			(0.0975)					
Predicted MII: KOF Index of Glob.				−0.0783				
				(0.0587)				
Predicted MII: Monetary freedom					−0.0628			
					(0.145)			
Predicted MII: Investment freedom						−0.220**		
						(0.106)		
Predicted MII: property rights							−0.187**	
							(0.0819)	
Predicted MII: All Institutional Det.								−0.201***
								(0.0581)
Constant	0.300***	1.050**	0.338***	0.250**	0.490***	0.132*	0.124*	0.188***
	(0.113)	(0.478)	(0.114)	(0.101)	(0.179)	(0.0708)	(0.0652)	(0.0438)
Observations	590	449	596	596	596	596	596	445

(continued)

Table 3.5 (continued)

Variables	(1)	(2)	(3)	(4)	(5)	(6)	(7)	(8)
Number of countries	42	44	44	44	44	44	44	42
Hansen OIR test	1.000	1.000	1.000	1.000	0.992	0.989	0.999	1.000
AR(1)	0.000690	0.137	0.000757	0.000647	0.000934	0.000508	0.000461	0.00858
AR(2)	0.158	0.103	0.144	0.141	0.143	0.156	0.111	0.216
AR(3)	0.118	0.0716	0.199	0.136	0.247	0.158	0.102	0.911

Note: Models (indicated by columns) estimated by System-GMM approach; in the parenthesis are robust standard errors ***$p < 0.01$, **$p < 0.05$, *$p < 0.1$. The null hypothesis of instrument set being valid exogenous is checked by the p-values of the Hansen Over-Identifying Restrictions (OIR) test. Arellano-Bond AR(1), AR(2) and AR(3) tests are used to check the null of no autocorrelation. To save space, time dummies not reported. Furthermore, all available lagged values of endogenous variables are used as instruments

Table 3.6 Dependent variable -real GDP- non-prolonged users

Variables	(1)	(2)	(3)	(4)	(5)	(6)	(7)	(8)
Lag Log Real GDP	1.002***	1.006***	1.003***	1.014***	0.982***	1.027***	0.925***	1.010***
	(0.00251)	(0.00888)	(0.00264)	(0.00971)	(0.0156)	(0.0106)	(0.0336)	(0.00514)
Log population	0.00136	0.00446	0.00202	0.00406	0.00368	0.00251	−0.0159	0.00882
	(0.00179)	(0.00313)	(0.00209)	(0.00345)	(0.00838)	(0.00664)	(0.0100)	(0.00793)
Government spending	−2.63e-05	0.000569	0.000111	0.000347	−0.00117	0.000249	−0.000221	0.000131
	(0.000144)	(0.000476)	(0.000158)	(0.000529)	(0.00113)	(0.000737)	(0.000757)	(0.000266)
Predicted MII: Regime & Military	−0.105***							
	(0.0299)							
Predicted MII: Agg. Gov. Ind.		−0.274***						
		(0.102)						
Predicted MII: Civil liberties			−0.0677*					
			(0.0367)					
Predicted MII: KOF Index of Glob.				−0.159*				
				(0.0905)				
Predicted MII: Monetary freedom					−0.677**			
					(0.295)			
Predicted MII: Investment freedom						−0.317*		
						(0.173)		
Predicted MII: Property rights							−0.0480	
							(0.143)	
Predicted MII: All Institutional Det.								−0.0414
								(0.126)
Constant	0.000395	−0.0347	−0.0480	−0.121	0.444	−0.154	0.876**	−0.190
	(0.0417)	(0.128)	(0.0516)	(0.127)	(0.312)	(0.154)	(0.407)	(0.116)
Observations	883	725	957	958	961	961	961	665

(continued)

Table 3.6 (continued)

Variables	(1)	(2)	(3)	(4)	(5)	(6)	(7)	(8)
Number of countries	70	77	75	77	77	77	77	69
Hansen OIR test	1.000	0.231	1.000	0.513	0.517	0.153	0.322	1.000
AR(1)	0.0430	0.0506	0.0439	0.0525	0.0458	0.0483	0.0563	0.103
AR(2)	0.0528	0.146	0.0439	0.0440	0.0153	0.0359	0.0515	0.205
AR(3)	0.202	0.309	0.182	0.181	0.220	0.169	0.186	0.361

Note: Models (indicated by columns) estimated by System-GMM approach; in the parenthesis are robust standard errors ***$p < 0.01$, **$p < 0.05$, *$p < 0.1$. The null hypothesis of instrument set being valid exogenous is checked by the p-values of the Hansen Over-Identifying Restrictions (OIR) test. Arellano-Bond AR(1), AR(2) and AR(3) tests are used to check the null of no autocorrelation. To save space, time dummies not reported. Furthermore, all available lagged values of endogenous variables are used as instruments

countries; while the negative impact remains insignificant in the case of non-programme countries. Moreover, civil liberties positively and significantly contribute in enhancing real GDP in the case of non-prolonged users (and the non-programme countries), while the positive impact remains insignificant in the case of prolonged users.

Aggregate governance indicator comes out to be highly important in enhancing real economic growth, since it holds significantly positive consequence for real GDP, for both the prolonged and non-prolonged users (and also in the case of non-programme countries).

The importance of openness of the economy is reflected in KOF index of globalization having a significantly positive impact on real GDP, for both the programme and non-programme countries. Also, monetary freedom significantly enhances real GDP for both the sub-groups (while the impact remains positive but insignificant in the case of non-programme countries).

At the same time while investment freedom holds a positive (though insignificant) consequence for real GDP in the case of non-prolonged users (and also the non-programme countries), it holds a significantly positive bearing on real GDP in the case of prolonged users.

Property rights play an important role in reducing transaction costs (that help enhance investment). Acemoglu and Johnson (2005, p. 953) pointed out that countries where institutions protected property rights more, performed better in terms of indictors related with investment, credit to private sector, stock markets, and income per capita. A similar result is pointed out by Acemoglu and Robinson (2012) in terms of Netherlands and UK paying greater attention to developing private property protection institutional framework, and in turn growing quicker than their neighbours. Having said that, estimated impact of property rights remain positive but insignificant on real GDP, for both the sub-groups. It may be possible that by strengthening the supporting institutional setup, the impact of property rights on real GDP could become more effective (or in other words, significant); since the variable of property rights has been estimated to be positively significant in the non-programme countries, which are overall more developed than the programme countries, in terms of their institutional setup.

Moreover, model (8) in which all institutional determinants have been taken together, indicates results, which are overall in line with the results of the individual models, although due to a lack of overall weak supporting institutional environment, certain institutional determinants (which individually remain positive and significant in enhancing real GDP) become insignificant in terms of their impact on real GDP. Hence, it is important that impact of institutional determinants is made stronger through enhanced focus on them and their supporting institutional environment.

The discussion will now move towards estimating and analysing Eq. (3.2) for the purpose of establishing the first part (i.e., institutional impact on MII) of the overall indirect effect of institutional determinants on real GDP through macroeconomic stability. Tables 3.3 and 3.4, once again highlight the presence of dynamic process, since lagged MII positively and significantly impacts current MII, for both the prolonged and non-prolonged users. The same consequence can be observed in the case of non-programme countries (see Table 3.9).

In the case of prolonged users, a military officer as chief executive significantly enhances MII. Moreover, the role of particular form of regime (parliamentary or presidential) remains insignificant in impacting MII.

Aggregate governance indicator remains negative, though insignificantly for MII in the case of both prolonged- and non-prolonged users; while the impact is significantly negative in the case of non-programme countries. Also, civil liberties hold a significantly negative consequence for prolonged users; while the impact remains insignificant in the case of non-prolonged users and non-programme countries.

Arpac et al. (2008), for instance, indicated that implementation record of IMF programmes was better in those programme countries, as compared to others, where the level of trade openness improved. Similarly, in the current study, it can be seen that an improvement in KOF index of globalization significantly reduces MII in both the sub-groups, highlighting the importance of openness here. Also, monetary freedom remains significantly negative in the case of prolonged users.

The situation of investment freedom is a bit complex, where estimated investment freedom significantly enhances MII in the case of non- prolonged users, while the impact remains significantly negative in the case of non-programme countries.

Hence, unlike non-programme countries where institutional mechanism is better established with regard to Investment freedom, absence of needed controls on Investment freedom for checking capital flight (for example the case of East Asian crisis of the 1990s) may be one of the weaknesses in the overall fiscal freedom environment that may have led to such an estimated positive consequence for MII; calling in turn, for augmenting pro-investment institutional setup in the case of non-prolonged users.

Property rights has an insignificantly negative consequence for MII in the case of prolonged- and non-prolonged users (and the non-programme countries), giving way to the argument that the supporting institutional framework needs to be strengthened to make the impact significant for MII.

Moreover, model (8) where all institutional determinants have been taken together, are although in line with the overall analysis, but many determinants here, which have otherwise remained individually significant for reducing MII, become insignificant due to the overall weak institutional supporting environment. Hence, it is important that impact of institutional determinants is made stronger through enhanced focus on them and their supporting institutional environment.

As can be seen in Tables 3.5 and 3.6 (and also Table 3.10), predicted MII in most of the cases impact negatively on real GDP; while in many cases the impact is significant, along with being negative. It can also be noted that while $\widehat{\text{MII}}$, determined on the basis of a combined effect of all the institutional determinants, is significantly negative for real GDP in the case of prolonged users, it also impacts real GDP negatively (though insignificantly) in the case of non-prolonged users (and non-programme countries).

Summing Up Results of Tables 3.1 and 3.2 are in line with the premise laid out in [a], which indicates that institutional determinants have an overall significantly positive effect on real GDP, for both the prolonged and non-prolonged users. At the same time, support for the second premise (as indicated in [b]) that institutional determinants negatively impact MII can be seen in the estimations reflected in Tables 3.3 and 3.4, where most of the institutional determinants have a negative effect on MII, while in certain cases, the impact becomes significantly negative. Lastly, the third premise (as indicated in [c]) that the predicted MII [estimated from institutional determinants in Eq. (3.2)] have a negative impact on real GDP, stands also supported by most of the estimations indicated by Tables 3.5 and 3.6. This, along with the fact that these institutional determinants in the first place are the ones that significantly impacted economic- and political institutional quality in programme countries during 1980–2009 (the same time period as of the current study).[20]

Overall, it would pertinent to indicate therefore, that the 'missing link' of institutions for reaching a positive economic growth consequence, does in fact exist in IMF programme countries. Hence, these significant institutional determinants need to be focused upon in future IMF programmes, since it can be seen that they positively affect real GDP both directly, and also indirectly through first negatively impacting MII, and then the predicted MII negatively affecting real GDP. Moreover, when the significant determinants of institutional quality for programme countries, were checked for their impact in the case of non-programme countries (during the same time period; see Tables 3.8, 3.9, and 3.10), the estimated results here also were in line with the three premise (indicated in the theoretical framework).

3.4.1 Robustness Check

Table 3.7 presents the estimated impact of MII on real GDP, indicating in turn that MII significantly and negatively impacts GDP and MII, in the case of both prolonged- and the non-prolonged users. This can be seen as a robustness check for estimations of real GDP and predicted MII (in Tables 3.5 and 3.6), where a negative relationship also exists in most of the cases. Moreover, Table 3.7 also indicates that MII significantly and negatively impacts real GDP in the case of non-programme countries, while the same relationship exists for the non-programme countries in most of the cases for predicted MII and real GDP (see Table 3.10).

[20] For details see Chap. 2.

Table 3.7 Dependent variable -real GDP- prolonged and non-prolonged users, and non-programme countries

Variables	(1) Prolonged Users	(2) Non-Prolonged Users	(3) Non-Programme Countries
Lag Log Real GDP	1.000***	0.714***	0.992***
	(0.00389)	(0.0760)	(0.00464)
Log population	−0.00467**	−0.0715***	−0.000549
	(0.00185)	(0.0274)	(0.00107)
Government spending	0.000418**	8.22e-05	−0.000214
	(0.000208)	(0.000179)	(0.000196)
MII	−0.0856***	−0.0759***	−0.0890***
	(0.0196)	(0.0125)	(0.0238)
Constant	0.0644	3.423***	0.202***
	(0.0400)	(0.965)	(0.0705)
Observations	596	963	612
Number of countries	44	77	51
Hansen OIR test	1.000	1.000	1.000
AR(1)	0.000562	0.0175	0.00127
AR(2)	0.103	0.0740	0.622
AR(3)	0.998	0.123	0.476

Note: Models (indicated by columns) estimated by System-GMM approach; in the parenthesis are robust standard errors ***$p < 0.01$, **$p < 0.05$, *$p < 0.1$. The null hypothesis of instrument set being valid exogenous is checked by the p-values of the Hansen Over-Identifying Restrictions (OIR) test. Arellano-Bond AR(1), AR(2) and AR(3) tests are used to check the null of no autocorrelation. To save space, time dummies not reported. Furthermore, all available lagged values of endogenous variables are used as instruments

3.5 Conclusion

The problem of a poor performance of IMF programmes in terms of economic growth in recipient countries on one hand, and NIE literature's highlighting the important role institutions play in enhancing economic growth in many countries, on the other, created in turn a 'missing link' that served as a motivation for the current study. The time duration of the study was 1980–2009, and the System-GMM approach was applied for carrying out the analysis. Subsequently, the estimated impact of institutional determinants (both political and economic) was found to be overall significant for enhancing real economic growth, both for prolonged- and non-prolonged users of IMF. At the same time, institutional determinants were also found to be overall significant in reducing macroeconomic instability. Moreover, predicted MII in turn also impacted negatively on real GDP. Hence, it has been pointed out that institutional determinants positively impacted real GDP both directly, as well as indirectly, through the channel of macroeconomic stability. The above estimations were carried out with institutional determinants, which in Chap. 2 were found to be significant in the programme countries. As an extension, when these significant institutional determinants were checked in the case of non-programme countries, similar estimated results were obtained, as in the case of programme countries.

Appendix

Table 3.8 Dependent variable -real GDP-non-programme countries

Variables	(1)	(2)	(3)	(4)	(5)	(6)	(7)	(8)
Lag Log Real GDP	0.976***	0.984***	0.981***	0.969***	0.938***	0.951***	0.944***	0.987***
	(0.00812)	(0.0199)	(0.00687)	(0.00900)	(0.0348)	(0.0108)	(0.0107)	(0.00379)
Log population	0.000704	−0.00137	−0.000686	−0.00275	−0.0651	0.00167	0.00202	0.000561
	(0.00243)	(0.00292)	(0.00151)	(0.00250)	(0.0428)	(0.00550)	(0.00518)	(0.00120)
Government spending	0.000221	−0.000641	−0.000334	−4.49e-05	−1.50e-05	0.000251	0.000228	−0.000200
	(0.000189)	(0.000564)	(0.000279)	(0.000202)	(0.000200)	(0.000210)	(0.000216)	(0.000138)
Regime	0.0455***							0.0123
	(0.0145)							(0.00961)
Military	−0.0206							0.00160
	(0.0216)							(0.0122)
Agg. Gov. Ind.		0.00130**						0.000476
		(0.000523)						(0.000419)
Civil liberties			0.00507***					−0.00368
			(0.00194)					(0.00250)
KOF Index of Glob.				0.00159***				−0.000310
				(0.000582)				(0.000406)
Monetary freedom					0.000253			0.000293
					(0.000220)			(0.000348)
Investment freedom						0.000121		4.91e-05
						(0.000293)		(0.000155)
Property rights							0.000801*	−0.000171
							(0.000482)	(0.000263)
Constant	0.167*	0.126	0.188**	0.236***	1.609**	0.420***	0.539***	0.140***
	(0.0900)	(0.143)	(0.0844)	(0.0860)	(0.650)	(0.113)	(0.107)	(0.0323)

(continued)

Table 3.8 (continued)

Variables	(1)	(2)	(3)	(4)	(5)	(6)	(7)	(8)
Observations	606	465	610	611	610	610	613	457
Number of countries	47	52	51	50	52	52	52	46
Hansen OIR test	1.000	1.000	1.000	1.000	1.000	1.000	1.000	1.000
AR(1)	0.00100	0.0154	0.000881	0.000959	0.00131	0.000863	0.00115	0.0216
AR(2)	0.465	0.202	0.729	0.566	0.618	0.524	0.576	0.188
AR(3)	0.465	0.0890	0.692	0.562	0.535	0.506	0.507	0.0784

Note: Models (indicated by columns) estimated by System-GMM approach; in the parenthesis are robust standard errors ***$p < 0.01$, **$p < 0.05$, *$p < 0.1$. Models taken separately to see impact of variables individually (along with avoiding collinearity issue among variables); last model includes all the variables and checks their impact taken together. The null hypothesis of instrument set being valid exogenous is checked by the p-values of the Hansen Over-Identifying Restrictions (OIR) test. Arellano-Bond AR(1), AR(2) and AR(3) tests are used to check the null of no autocorrelation. To save space, time dummies not reported. Furthermore, all available lagged values of endogenous variables are used as instruments

Table 3.9 Dependent variable -MII- non-programme countries

Variables	(1)	(2)	(3)	(4)	(5)	(6)	(7)	(8)
Lag MII	0.558***	0.641***	0.648***	0.538***	0.704***	0.699***	0.734***	0.439***
	(0.0332)	(0.125)	(0.0328)	(0.0299)	(0.0669)	(0.0707)	(0.0607)	(0.0950)
Regime	0.0570							0.358
	(0.0424)							(0.622)
Military	−0.0140							−0.378
	(0.0284)							(1.478)
Agg. Gov. Ind.		−0.00484*						−0.0134***
		(0.00267)						(0.00445)
Civil liberties			0.00330					−0.00505
			(0.00257)					(0.0594)
KOF Index of Glob.				−0.000446				−0.00383
				(0.000769)				(0.0134)
Monetary freedom					−0.000416			0.00254
					(0.000992)			(0.00222)
Investment freedom						−0.00173*		0.00332
						(0.00103)		(0.00220)
Property rights							−0.000596	−0.00116
							(0.00118)	(0.00214)
Constant	0.225***	0.457***	0.200***	0.293***	0.241***	0.312***	0.152**	−0.500
	(0.0274)	(0.170)	(0.0211)	(0.0510)	(0.0680)	(0.0648)	(0.0707)	(1.726)
Observations	1316	596	1418	1382	635	635	637	474
Number of countries	49	55	54	52	52	52	52	47
Hansen OIR test	1.000	0.200	1.000	1.000	0.703	0.861	0.969	1.000

(continued)

Table 3.9 (continued)

Variables	(1)	(2)	(3)	(4)	(5)	(6)	(7)	(8)
AR(1)	7.45e-07	0.000712	3.07e-07	3.12e-07	6.07e-06	2.87e-06	7.63e-06	2.52e-05
AR(2)	0.675	0.399	0.961	0.762	0.309	0.335	0.288	0.659
AR(3)	0.180	0.297	0.783	0.502	0.493	0.564	0.498	0.750

Note: Models (indicated by columns) estimated by System-GMM approach; in the parenthesis are robust standard errors ***$p < 0.01$, **$p < 0.05$, *$p < 0.1$. Models taken separately to see impact of variables individually (along with avoiding collinearity issue among variables); last model includes all the variables and checks their impact taken together. The null hypothesis of instrument set being valid exogenous is checked by the p-values of the Hansen Over-Identifying Restrictions (OIR) test. Arellano-Bond AR(1), AR(2) and AR(3) tests are used to check the null of no autocorrelation. To save space, time dummies not reported. Furthermore, all available lagged values of endogenous variables are used as instruments

Table 3.10 Dependent variable -real GDP-non-programme countries

Variables	(1)	(2)	(3)	(4)	(5)	(6)	(7)	(8)
Lag Log Real GDP	0.944***	0.976***	0.989***	0.985***	0.983***	0.988***	0.982***	1.029***
	(0.0340)	(0.00793)	(0.00593)	(0.00656)	(0.00517)	(0.00702)	(0.0103)	(0.0884)
Log population	−0.0603	−0.000369	−0.000547	−0.00115	−0.000736	−0.00356	−0.00316	−0.0658*
	(0.0412)	(0.00160)	(0.00112)	(0.00136)	(0.00134)	(0.00462)	(0.00528)	(0.0392)
Government spending	−8.42e-05	−0.000410	−0.000379	−0.000340	−0.000285	−0.000442	−0.000270	−0.000375
	(0.000202)	(0.000342)	(0.000252)	(0.000245)	(0.000220)	(0.000284)	(0.000244)	(0.000382)
Predicted MII: Regime & Military	−0.0433**							
	(0.0220)							
Predicted MII: Agg. Gov. Ind.		−0.126***						
		(0.0342)						
Predicted MII: Civil liberties			−0.0839***					
			(0.0270)					
Predicted MII: KOF Index of Glob.				−0.113***				
				(0.0309)				
Predicted MII: Monetary freedom					−0.171**			
					(0.0798)			
Predicted MII: Investment freedom						−0.163***		
						(0.0445)		
Predicted MII: Property rights							−0.0402	
							(0.0479)	
Predicted MII: All Institutional Det.								−0.281
								(0.297)
Constant	1.492**	0.307***	0.180**	0.286***	0.228***	0.242*	0.265	2.023
	(0.675)	(0.0926)	(0.0744)	(0.0966)	(0.0827)	(0.133)	(0.166)	(2.394)
Observations	605	464	608	610	609	609	611	457

(continued)

Table 3.10 (continued)

Variables	(1)	(2)	(3)	(4)	(5)	(6)	(7)	(8)
Number of countries	47	51	50	50	51	51	51	46
Hansen OIR test	1.000	1.000	1.000	1.000	1.000	1.000	1.000	0.992
AR(1)	0.00104	0.0166	0.00101	0.000957	0.00105	0.000799	0.000890	0.0191
AR(2)	0.593	0.222	0.774	0.754	0.895	0.805	0.693	0.215
AR(3)	0.625	0.0990	0.732	0.718	0.583	0.767	0.668	0.0423

Note: Models (indicated by columns) estimated by System-GMM approach; in the parenthesis are robust standard errors ***$p < 0.01$, **$p < 0.05$, *$p < 0.1$. The null hypothesis of instrument set being valid exogenous is checked by the p-values of the Hansen Over-Identifying Restrictions (OIR) test. Arellano-Bond AR(1), AR(2) and AR(3) tests are used to check the null of no autocorrelation. To save space, time dummies not reported. Furthermore, all available lagged values of endogenous variables are used as instruments

Table 3.11 Group-wise list of IMF member countries

Non-programme countries			
Australia	France	Montenegro	Spain
Austria	Germany	Myanmar	Suriname
Bahamas	Greece	Namibia	Swaziland
Bahrain	Republic of Islamic Iran	Netherlands	Sweden
Belgium	Ireland	New Zealand	Switzerland
Bhutan	Italy	Nigeria	Syrian Arab Republic
Botswana	Japan	Norway	Timor-Leste
Brunei Darussalam	Kiribati	Oman	Tonga
Canada	Kuwait	Palau	Turkmenistan
Colombia	Libya	Paraguay	Tuvalu
Cyprus	Luxembourg	Qatar	United Arab Emirates
Denmark	Malaysia	San Marino	United Kingdom
El Salvador	Malta	Saudi Arabia	United States
Eritrea	Marshall Islands	Singapore	Vanuatu
Finland	Federated States of Micronesia	South Sudan	
Programme countries			
Non-prolonged users			
Afghanistan	Djibouti	Republic of Korea	Solomon Islands
Angola	Ecuador	Kosovo	Somalia
Antigua and Barbuda	Republic of Arab Egypt	Latvia	Spain
Republic of Azerbaijan	Equatorial Guinea	Lebanon	Sri Lanka
Bangladesh	Republic of Estonia	Lesotho	St. Kitts and Nevis
Barbados	Ethiopia	Liberia	St. Lucia
Belarus	Fiji	Republic of Lithuania	St. Vincent and the Grenadines
Belize	Gabon	Maldives	Syrian Arab Republic
Bosnia and Herzegovina	Gambia	Mauritius	Thailand
Brazil	Grenada	Moldova	Togo
Cambodia	Guatemala	Morocco	Trinidad and Tobago
Cape Verde	Guinea-Bissau	Nepal	Tunisia
Central African Republic	Haiti	Papua New Guinea	Ukraine
Chile	Hungary	Peru	Uruguay
China	Iceland	Poland	Uzbekistan
Comoros	India	Portugal	República Bolivariana de Venezuela
Democratic Republic of the Congo	Indonesia	Romania	Vietnam
Republic of Congo	Iraq	Samoa	Republic of Yemen
Costa Rica	Israel	Serbia	Zimbabwe
Cyprus	Jamaica	Singapore	

(continued)

Table 3.11 (continued)

Czech Republic	Republic of Kazakhstan	Slovak Republic	
Côte d'Ivoire	Kenya	Slovenia	
Prolonged users			
Albania	Dominica	Madagascar	Philippines
Algeria	Dominican Republic	Malawi	Russian Federation
Argentina	Georgia	Mali	Rwanda
Armenia	Ghana	Mauritania	Senegal
Benin	Guinea	Mexico	Serbia
Bolivia	Guyana	Mongolia	Sierra Leone
Bulgaria	Honduras	Mozambique	Tajikistan
Burkina Faso	Jordan	Nicaragua	Tanzania
Burundi	Kyrgyz Republic	Niger	Turkey
Cameroon	Lao People's Democratic Republic	Pakistan	Uganda
Chad	Macedonia	Panama	Zambia

Note: Countries are listed in alphabetical order. Also, the groups correspond to the time period of 1980–2009

References

Abbott P, Barnebeck T, Tarp F (2010) IMF and economic reform in developing countries. Q Rev Econ Finance 50:17–26

Acemoglu D, Johnson S (2005) Unbundling institutions. J Polit Econ 113:949–995

Acemoglu D, Robinson JA (2012) Why nations fail: the origins of power, prosperity, and poverty, 1st edn. Crown Business, New York, NY

Acemoglu D, Johnson S, Robinson J (2001) The colonial origins of comparative development: an empirical investigation. Am Econ Rev 91:1369–1401

Acemoglu D, Johnson S, Robinson J (2003a) An African success: Botswana. In: Rodrik D (ed) In search of prosperity: analytic narratives on economic growth, 2nd edn. Princeton University Press, Princeton, NJ

Acemoglu D, Johnson S, Robinson J, Thaicharoen Y (2003b) Institutional causes, macroeconomic symptoms: volatility, crises and growth. J Monet Econ 50:49–123

Acemoglu D, Johnson S, Robinson J (2004) Institutions as the fundamental cause of long-run growth. NBER working paper no 10481. NBER, Cambridge, MA

Afonso A, Jalles JT (2011) Economic performance and government size. ECB working paper series no 1399. ECB, Germany

Arellano M, Bover O (1995) Another look at instrumental variables estimation of error-component models. J Econ 68:29–51

Arpac O, Bird G, Mandilaras A (2008) Stop interrupting: an empirical analysis of the implementation of IMF programs. World Dev 36:1493–1513

Barro RJ, Lee J (2005) IMF programs: who is chosen and what are the effects? J Monet Econ 52:1245–1269

Bird G (1996) Borrowing from the IMF: the policy implications of recent empirical research. World Dev 24:1753–1760

Bird G (2001) IMF programs: do they work? Can they be made to work better? World Dev 29:1849–1865

Bird G (2007) The IMF: a bird's eye view of its role and operations. J Econ Surv 21:683–745

Bird G, Willett T (2004) IMF conditionality, implementation and the new political economy of ownership. Comp Econ Stud 46:423–450
Blundell R, Bond S (1998) Initial conditions and moment restrictions in dynamic panel data models. J Econ 87:115–143
Buira A (1983) IMF financial programs and conditionality. J Dev Econ 12:111–136
Butkiewicz JL, Yanikkaya H (2005) The effects of IMF and World Bank lending on long-run economic growth: an empirical analysis. World Dev 33:371–391
Conway P (2006) The International Monetary Fund in a time of crisis: a review of Stanley Fischer's IMF essays from a time of crisis: The international financial system, stabilization, and development. J Econ Lit 44:115–144
Donovan D (1981) Real responses associated with exchange-rate action in selected upper credit tranche stabilization programs. IMF staff papers no 698-727. IMF, Washington, DC
Dreher A (2006) IMF and economic growth: the effects of programs, loans, and compliance with conditionality. World Dev 34:769–788
Easterly W (2005) What did structural adjustment adjust? The association of policies and growth with repeated IMF and World Bank adjustment loans. J Dev Econ 76:1–22
Evrensel AY (2002) Effectiveness of IMF-supported stabilization programs in developing countries. J Int Money Finance 21:565–587
Goldstein M, Montiel P (1986) Evaluating fund stabilization programs with multi-country data: some methodological pitfalls. IMF staff papers no 304–344. IMF, Washington, DC
Haghighi AK, Sameti M, Isfahani RD (2012) The effect of macroeconomic instability on economic growth in Iran. Res Appl Econ 4:39–61
Hall RE, Jones CI (1999) Why do some countries produce so much more output per worker than others? Q J Econ 114:83–116
Hansen LP (1982) Large sample properties of generalized method of moments estimators. Econometrica 50:1029–1054
Hutchison MM, Noy I (2003) Macroeconomic effects of IMF-sponsored programs in Latin America: output costs, program recidivism and the vicious cycle of failed stabilizations. J Int Money Finance 22:991–1014
IEO/IMF (2007) An IEO evaluation of structural conditionality in IMF-supported programs. IMF, Washington, DC
IMF (2005) Building institutions. In: World Economic Outlook, Building Institutions, World Economic and financial surveys. IMF, Washington, DC, pp 125–160
Ismihan M (2003) The role of politics and instability and public spending dynamics and macroeconomic performance: theory and evidence from Turkey. PhD thesis. METU, Ankara
Kaufmann D, Kraay A, Mastruzzi M (2010) The worldwide governance indicators: methodology and analytical issues. World Bank policy research working paper no. 5430. The World Bank, Washington, DC
Khan MS (1990) The macroeconomic effects of fund-supported adjustment programs. IMF staff papers no 195–231. IMF, Washington, DC
Khan MS, Knight MD (1981) Stabilization programs in developing countries: a formal framework. IMF staff papers no 1–53. IMF, Washington, DC
Khan MS, Knight MD (1985) Fund supported adjustment programs and economic growth. IMF Occasional papers no 41. IMF, Washington, DC
Killick T, Malik M, Manuel M (1992) What can we know about the effects of IMF programmes? World Econ 15:575–598
Loxley J (1984) The IMF and the poorest countries, 1st edn. North-South Institute, Ottawa
Nsouli SM, Atoian R, Mourmouras A (2004) Institutions, program implementation, and macroeconomic performance. IMF working paper no 04-184. IMF, Washington, DC
Parsons QN, Robinson JA (2006) State formation and governance in Botswana. J Afr Econ 15:100–140
Pastor M (1987) The effects of IMF programs in the third world: debate and evidence from Latin America. World Dev 15:249–262

Przeworski A, Vreeland JR (2000) The effect of IMF programs on economic growth. J Dev Econ 62:385–421

Rodrik D, Subramanian A, Trebbi F (2002) Institutions rule: the primacy of institutions over geography and integration in economic development. Centre for Economic Policy Research discussion paper series no 3643. Centre for Economic Policy Research, London

Roodman D (2007) A short note on the theme of too many instruments. Center for Global Development working papers 125. Center for Global Development, Washington, DC

Ugur M (2010) Institutions and economic performance: a review of the theory and evidence. MPRA Paper 25909. University Library of Munich, Munich. http://mpra.ub.uni-muenchen.de/25909/. Accessed 10 Nov 2013

Ul Haque N, Khan MS (1998) Do IMF-supported programs work? A survey of the cross-country empirical evidence. IMF working paper no 98/169. IMF, Washington, DC

von Hagen J (1991) A note on the empirical effectiveness of formal fiscal restraints. J Public Econ 44:99–110

Chapter 4
IMF Programmes and Institutional Quality Determinants: Economic Scenarios in Pakistan

Abstract Pakistan has been selected in this chapter as a representative example of a frequent user of IMF resources. Here, by applying the Vector Autoregression (VAR) model techniques, various counterfactual scenarios are estimated for a period of 1980–2014, to see impact of a significant institutional determinant (from Chap. 2), KOF index of globalization on macroeconomic instability and real economic growth. Results highlight that through enhanced focus on institutional quality determinants, macroeconomic instability can be reduced, and hence higher growth rate of GDP can be achieved.

4.1 Introduction

Pakistan has been a prolonged user[1] of IMF resources since the late 1980s. From Table 2.1 (in Chap. 2), it could be seen that during 1980–2009, Pakistan was one of the 44 prolonged users; remaining under IMF programmes for half of those 30 years (where Mali and Senegal were at the top with 23 years each during the time period taken). Moreover, Pakistan remained a prolonged user during both the decades of 1990s and 2000s. Even after being a prolonged user it could not achieve sustained macroeconomic stabilization, while yearly economic growth on average since 1980s was substantially lower than that of the two decades before it (IEO 2002, pp. 119–121).

Although, Article I, clause (v) of the Articles of Agreement of the International Monetary Fund[2] indicates that resources will be made available to members on a 'temporary' basis, it is ironic that since 1988 Pakistan has entered more than 12 IMF programmes (and currently is in the 'Extended Fund Facility' (EFF)[3] IMF programme); while the programme completion rate has been abysmally low, as only one of the programmes so far has been able to meet the macroeconomy related

[1] According to IEO (2002, p. 9 and 24) a country is considered to be a prolonged user if during a decade it remains for at least seven years in an IMF programme.

[2] http://www.imf.org/external/pubs/ft/aa/pdf/aa.pdf

[3] https://www.imf.org/external/np/exr/facts/eff.htm

O. Javed, *The Economic Impact of International Monetary Fund Programmes*, Contributions to Economics, DOI 10.1007/978-3-319-29178-9_4

targets (Ahmad and Mohammed 2012)! The fact that Pakistan has been able to get frequent IMF financial support underlines not only the recidivist behaviour but also raises questions about the IMF's criteria behind negotiating future programmes with recipient countries that had poor programme implementation record. Having said that this easy availability of money appears to have allowed successive governments to continuously postpone undertaking hard reforms, and this lack of political will to implement the reform agenda negotiated with the IMF, exists as one of the reasons behind the poor performance under the programmes, in terms of macroeconomic stability and economic growth.

Notwithstanding the fact that many programmes went off-track in the early stages, the rigid, one-size-fits-all kind of programme conditionalities overly squeezed the demand side to meet certain macroeconomic targets, without being able to focus on the supply side enough to have positive consequences for economic growth. Moreover, the underlying Neo-Classical behavioural assumptions of the programme design saw a world of no transaction costs, and hence not much role of institutions. The fact that institutional environment could neither be focused upon or prioritized in the scope and sequencing of conditionalities, meant programme neglect towards enhancing the underlying political and economic institutional determinants like lack of appropriate level of governance, property rights protection, and freedoms that provide a conducive environment for economic activity and its regulation.

NIE literature, on the other hand, has pointed towards substantial empirical evidence in the last three decades or so, indicating that countries, which focused on improving determinants of institutional quality witnessed sustained macroeconomic stability and economic growth.

Given this background, I intend to conduct counterfactual simulation analysis for Pakistan, which is a representative prolonged user, since it has been one of the most frequent users of IMF resources, and which has not been able to attain either sustained macroeconomic stability or positive consequences for economic growth. More specifically I will backcast the time series data of Pakistan by redesigning the IMF programme, in which, the traditional Fund approach is combined with the framework of NIE. I will look at: 'Had Fund's programme been designed to focus on strengthening institutions then what would have been the impact on macroeconomic stability and economic growth of Pakistan?' This analysis, by redesigning the Fund's policies through enhanced focus on strengthening institutions, is expected to bring sustained positive long-term consequences for macroeconomic stability and economic growth.

Outline of the study is as follows: literature will be reviewed in Sect. 4.2, institutional analysis of Pakistan will be taken up in Sect. 4.3, data and methodology will be discussed in Sect. 4.4, followed by discussion of estimation and results in Sect. 4.5. The study will be concluded in Sect. 4.6.

4.2 Literature Review

IEO (2002, p. 119) pointed out that Pakistan's yearly economic growth was on average around 6–7 % during the 1970s to the later part of 1980s, and the country was able to sustain its deficits in the fiscal and external sectors, without needing any major foreign assistance. This situation changed during late 1980s when economic growth started to deteriorate and inability to deal successfully with deficits led to build up of debt. Hence, the country entered successive IMF programmes in the years to follow, starting around the later part of 1980s.

Looking back, the experience proved to be worse in terms of yearly economic growth during 1988–2000, which on average stood at around a little less than 4 %, while at the same time major macroeconomic indicators, for example, inflation rate, foreign direct investment, export growth, and import cover in terms of foreign exchange reserves, all slacked when compared to the earlier two decades (IEO 2002, pp. 119–121). Since 2000, the situation has not changed much in terms of sustained macroeconomic stability and economic growth, although Pakistan continues to rely on IMF resources (with only an absence of few years during mid 2000s). Weaknesses in the rigid IMF's FPP framework, as shown by Killick (1995) and others, the limitations of the programme design to address the underlying institutional problems, along with easily available IMF finances, even at the back of low programme completion rates by Pakistan, could not allow the country to achieve sustained macroeconomic stabilization and economic growth.

The importance of focusing on institutional determinants could be seen from the fact that once a governance variable was focused upon in prolonged users, any difference in economic outlook between them and the non-prolonged users became insignificant (IEO 2002, p. 98). Yet institutional determinants were not focused upon as such in IMF programmes. Pakistan was no exception. Kemal (2003) pointed out that the (low) level of institutional quality deteriorated further since the early 1970s; with most deterioration happening in the 1990s. Greater institutional focus was all the more important since the quality of institutional determinants was quite on the lower side (when compared with other countries) as indicated by the ranking of Pakistan for many indicators of institutional quality (Khawaja and Khan 2011, p. 810).

IMF programmes, which are basically built on Polak model (Polak 1957), primarily try to fix Balance of Payments imbalances (and indirectly the fiscal imbalance of the government) by targeting monetary aggregates. But here too critics, including Killick (1995, p. 133), indicate that by focusing too much on monetary aggregates targeting, programmes are more tilted on the quantitative aspects and do not pay much attention to the qualitative basis of the reform agenda. Internalizing this criticism, IMF did try to enhance the scope of programmes by including more supply side initiatives, but the inability of the Fund to move away from the neo-classical/monetarist assumptions that have been shown by NIE literature to be quite out of sync with how the economies generally work (Groenewegen et al. 2010, pp. 13–24), has therefore not allowed IMF programmes to include much needed institutional focus and thus have not overall witnessed improved programme impacts.

Pakistan's high programme incompletion rate may be due to the underlying behavioural assumptions of IMF programmes (as indicated above) that have served as a disincentive for recipient countries, especially the prolonged users/developing countries that would, otherwise, see themselves more aligned to a world as depicted by the assumptions of NIE. Another reason may be the easy availability of IMF resources at the back of incomplete programmes by recipient countries. Incompetent governments have seen this as an opportunity to either follow some initial programme conditionalities to get the first few financial installments from IMF, and then leave the programme, and then start another programme after a little while to repeat the same; all this to postpone doing the hard economic reforms at the back of easily and frequently available IMF resources. This has worked as a moral hazard and has set in recidivist behaviour.

IMF has assumed in its programmes a high level of policy implementation of the conditionalities. In the wake of overall weak institutional environment in programme countries, where the situation is much worse on average in the case of prolonged users, expecting a high implementation rate of programme conditionalities has been over-ambitious from IMF to say the least. This is because, in the case of prolonged users like Pakistan, in particular, such a high level of implementation has seen to be missing due to the weak institutional environment, resulting in poor implementation of programme conditionalities. For example, starting from the very monetary sector, programme design assumes a predictable and stable demand of money in the economy (Killick 1995, p. 132), but in a weak institutional environment of programme countries in general and prolonged users (like Pakistan) in particular, such assumptions are overly restrictive and unrealistic. Even forecasting the underlying variability in circulation in income velocity lacks much precision, and hence reduces programme objectivity/implementation record with relation to monetary aggregates targeting.

The underlying Neo-Classical/Monetarist basis of programme design falls short of understanding the domestic environment particularly of the prolonged users, which are mostly developing countries. One attribute is the opportunistic behaviour whereby satisfying self-interest does not always lead to overall welfare gain in the society, as otherwise alluded to in the metaphor of 'invisible hand' (Groenewegen et al. 2010, p. 15). In fact, the political- and economic institutions collude to serve their own vested interests and therefore establish an 'extractive' institutional setup, which results in extraction of resources from the many to the group(s) that forms this collusion (Acemoglu and Robinson 2012, pp. 74–82; Acemoglu 2006; Acemoglu and Robinson 2008).[4] The incentive system in such an institutional

[4] 'Inclusive economic institutions' on the other hand, work towards and facilitate participation of people in economic activity. Moreover, an inclusive/extractive economic institution results because of an inclusive/extractive political institutional setup (Acemoglu and Robinson 2012, pp. 74–82; Acemoglu 2006; Acemoglu and Robinson 2008).

setup does not promote competition, but rather rewards behaviour that is loyal to sustaining this extractive institutional arrangement. This goes against the spirit of perfect competition, since the price signal that comes out of the market favours a certain lobby or individual, rather than being a natural outcome of true competition between buyers and sellers. These equilibrium market prices are sub-optimal and hence do not result in the optimal allocation of resources. In such a collusive institutional environment, markets no longer produce Pareto efficiency,[5] and as has been in the case of prolonged users like Pakistan, there are gross productive and allocative inefficiencies. In turn, it is therefore hard to see in developing countries like Pakistan much automatic clearing of markets and contracts being enforced, an active role of regulation (privately and through government), and existence of firms, in addition to markets, providing safeguards through governance structures that come about through institutions. Hence, IMF programmes need to move away to a NIE framework whose assumptions are cognizant of all these much probable possibilities, which are very much present in countries like Pakistan, and therefore underline the importance of institutions.

Moreover, IMF programmes not only lack focus on allocative and productive efficiencies (aspects of static efficiency) but also on features pertaining to dynamic efficiency. Internalizing the concept of dynamic efficiency by IMF would entail enhancing the scope of its programmes to focus on innovation, and the various linkages and elements that enable to reach it. This would mean coming up with programme conditionalities that lower the risks that entrepreneurs face by focusing on the role of government, by improving the environment that ensures enforceability of contracts and effectively assigns and enforces property rights (Groenewegen et al. 2010, pp. 16–17).

IMF programmes also need to internalize that achieving static and dynamic efficiencies entail bearing transaction costs, and that they add to production costs, and overall impact economic growth of a country. In countries like Pakistan, where a lot of information asymmetries exist, and where weak governance, poor enforceability of contracts and property rights, has led to high level of transaction costs. In this regard, North (1994, p. 360) pointed out that institutions matter when doing transactions that entail high costs.

In the case of extractive nature of institutions in Pakistan (Khawaja and Khan 2011, p. 810), IMF programmes need an enhanced scope to introduce conditionalities (mutually agreed between IMF and national authorities) that lower transaction costs in the case of firstly, market transactions that Commons (1931) referred to as 'bargaining transactions' between individuals that sell and buy at the market level. Secondly, the costs with regard to managerial transactions between superiors and subordinates at the organizational level also need to be made optimal. Lastly, political transactions at the level of authorities need to be brought into the scope of IMF programmes, so that property rights, taxes, and positive incentives are

[5] In such a situation, welfare of one person can only be increased by decreasing someone else's welfare (Groenewegen et al. 2010, p. 16).

provided in such a way that the related transaction costs get rationalized and that distribution of national wealth gets done optimally.

Libecap (1989) indicated that literature points out that the way property rights are allocated strongly determine the power distribution in the society. Allocation of property rights in a way that a group has great control results in the formulation of institutions that helps them gain immense power with the passage of time, raises a discussion to correct this unjustified initial distribution of property rights through an institutional reform effort (Groenewegen et al., 2010, pp. 130–131). In the case of Pakistan, inordinate distribution of land (mainly agricultural) among a select few locals was made by the British during the time of colonization, in return for this beneficiary group to offer services, which included, controlling local populations (that worked on these lands as peasants or labourers, and also influencing the nearby small land holders by putting weight on them by their sheer immense size of presence) from starting any rebellion against the colonizers. Hence, such a distribution of property rights allowed these groups to gain a lot of power and influence, since many people in the shape of peasants and labourers generally, became reliant for their livelihoods on them, and also earning from the produce of land gave this group a significant material/financial edge compared to many others in the society. This initial distribution of property rights was artificially done, since the recipient of such property rights did not otherwise have any natural claim (in terms of inheritance or personal monetary means) to justify such a grant of rights. This distribution put in place not only too much land in the hands of few individuals or families, which after the independence from British (resulting in the formation of Pakistan) were left with a lot of control and power in society to manipulate institutions so as to perpetuate their power ever further. In an independent Pakistan, these powerful political and economic elites colluded together to evolve political- and economic institutions in an extractive way [transferring resources from the many (the masses) to the few (the elites)], and hence achieved greater perpetuation of their power and reaped larger material gains over time. Hussain (1999) and Khawaja and Khan (2009, p. 18) also pointed towards this extractive behaviour of elites in Pakistan.

Therefore, IMF programmes not only need to focus on institutional determinants, but also need to help programme countries like Pakistan, move towards inclusive institutions. One of the ways for IMF to do this, is to base the programmes more on the framework of NIE, which does not leave most of interaction of agents in the economy on market forces alone, but rather acknowledges the importance of institutions at the back of the realization that agent's rationality is bounded, that opportunistic behaviour can exist to safeguard vested interests, that transaction costs exist, that there is a need to enforce contracts (more so in an ever increasing environment of impersonal exchange) and that an environment is needed for optimal allocation and adequate safeguard of property rights.

IMF programmes by basing its programmes on Neo-Classical/Monetarist behavioural assumptions, have basically seen macroeconomic issues, mainly the BOP imbalance, as a consequence of not properly targeting of monetary aggregates by the recipient country. In this sense, it limited its scope by mainly focusing on the demand side of the economy, while putting less emphasis on the institutional determinants (on the supply side), which have been shown in literature to play an equally important role in positively impacting macroeconomic stability and economic growth (Khan and Knight 1985; Acemoglu et al. 2003). NIE framework underlines the importance of focusing on institutional determinants as they are important for improving income per capita (Acemoglu and Johnson 2005; Afonso and Jalles 2011). Therefore, it seems appropriate for IMF programmes to constructively address criticism on programme design by adopting NIE framework. In doing so, it is hoped that the important role institutional determinants play for macroeconomic stability and economic growth, will be realized by the Fund.

4.3 Institutional Analysis of Pakistan: A NIE Perspective

4.3.1 Tracing the Political Economy

Pakistan has remained a developing country since its independence around 70 years ago. It has had development strategies that at one time during the 1960s favoured a centralized planned model for economy, where government tried to crowd-in the private sector, opposite of which happened in the next decade, while since the 1980s there has been an inconsistent policy, resulting in biased (in the face of vested interests of the elites) and inefficient moves towards liberalization, which lacked safeguarding the real vulnerable sectors, along with carrying out ill-designed and wrongly prioritized privatization/deregulation exercises; leaving the private sector poorly provided for to make and sustain financial and technical investments, and improperly regulated at the same time.

Pakistan enjoyed high growth rates during different times in its history. Yet these spells of growth could not be sustained over long periods of time. The underlying reason was existence of poor institutional quality, in fact, a result of extractive institutions as a colonial legacy, which only got perpetuated after the birth of the independent country through the politico-economic elite collusion. NIE indicates that low institutional quality has more to do with macroeconomic instability and volatility in the economy than the traditionally identified macroeconomic causes, which are in turn only symptoms of the deeper institutional problems (Acemoglu et al. 2003). Absence of inclusive institutions has meant few institutions to safeguard the vulnerable, to induce saving and investment, and to first of all educate the minds so that the mental constructs could negate the backward path dependencies, enable reliance of people on state rather than elites through educational and economic empowerment. Yet lack of this initiative, purposefully by the elites, meant growth spurts for a few years at the back of external borrowing, and not effective institutional setup that could bring sustained growth through creating a balanced and meaningful focus on the demand- and supply side factors. IMF programmes rather than unlocking the potential of supply side factors, squeezed the economy through over emphasis on demand side factors that further hurt the already weak investment and economic growth situation. Lack of sustained growth, at the back of extractive institutions meant that neither the benefits of regional trade (a geography related factor) could be realized, nor the economic benefits from exploring/extracting natural resources could be obtained. Therefore, economic success stories in time have overall remained marginal in terms of their impact, since they have not allowed the country to move up from the situation of low-growth equilibrium. Moreover, the IMF programmes have also not brought in sustained stability or positive growth consequences.

Vested interest groups, in the shape of collusion of political and economic elites, have tussled over power, with military although bringing some sanity by sidelining these vested groups, such stability was extremely transitory and would soon be fleeting. After coming into power, military would also start to make or help bring politicians in power from the existing lot in the country, given they supported them in legitimizing their Martial Law regimes. These political groups were given the status of second-in-command, that is, during military rule. Moreover, the military in power (mainly the top most brass) also went on institutionalizing extractive measures through colluding with their own chosen set of political- and economic elites.

The initiation of the above was a result of extractive nature of colonial experience before independence that left the newly independent country with a weak institutional setup. The outcome of governance so far has only caused the institutional setup to further weaken. Undercurrents of all this suggest that 'chaos' seems to help in the extractive ways of the elites. This chaos is retained and perpetuated by the elites to keep the people under-educated and economically dependent on elites than the state itself. Moreover, the situation has played very well into the hands of political elites who by creating this environment have overall remained successful in buying votes of people, without much performance otherwise. This has also raised questions on the country not meeting the pre-requisites of Westminster model of representative democracy, two of those mentioned above, pointing towards the need of changing the model of democracy which allows true public representation to surface from elections (and which may in time transition to a model similar to or exactly like the Westminster model, as the conditions of such a model in terms of its pre-requisites are met), and only those survive another election with the worry to win through performance than coercion and money.

4.3.2 *Defining the Actors in the Political Economy*

In IMF programmes, the recipient country in negotiation for the loan is referred to as the 'authorities'. On the face of it, by authorities is meant the Ministry of Finance and the State (or central) Bank (in the case of Pakistan, and similarly for other programme countries), yet the decision making flows from the influence of the elites. These elites are both the political ones in parliament, and their collaborators in the shape of economic elites, who help them from election financing to extracting resources, and in turn themselves reap the rewards of lopsided institutional matrix created by the political elites (about which I will discuss later). These political and economic elites in Pakistan have been people with deep agricultural, industrial, and/or financial base. Traditionally the base was mostly feudal, but with the passage of time, with long-term possession of political power and agricultural income and wealth, the elites moved to establish industrial base, and through exclusive inside information and lopsided favours from their economic collaborators/elites, like which stocks or projects to invest in or in the shape of loan write-offs from banks, political elites became well established in the financial- and real estate markets. Military in power also became a part of such vested interest groups of elites, and reaped similar kinds of benefits. Having said, weak writ of law and its application is yet to prove the above claims in a court of law. These elites together form the powerful actor in the economy in terms of their ability to influence informal institutions and make rules or formal institutions. This group as a whole may be called the 'limelight/active actor'. By perpetuating extractive institutions, they have been able to find ways to retain and perpetuate their position, and eventually as a whole contribute very little to the overall tax revenue.

In Pakistan then there is a group of small businessmen and salaried class in the urban centres, and small farmers in the rural setting, who are a big group of people, the main citizenry, and as a group may be referred to as the 'docile actor' since they have little control over policy. They are the main component of what makes the tax base in the economy.

Then there is a third kind of actor who runs the black economy. They pay virtually no taxes (only some indirect taxes) and in such may be called the 'invisible actor' as a whole. In the absence of VAT (Value-Added Tax), which applies to the entire supply chain, although they are not in the income tax net due to lack of documentation in the economy, they continue to contribute to businesses, which are otherwise in the tax net, as skilled labour or provider of raw materials. Hence, overall they are able to earn income/profit without paying any tax on it.

Due to high transaction costs involved in setting up a business (including costs related with corruption and nepotism), a part of invisible actor group although has entrepreneurial skills, works informally, that is does not register with the government. In that sense they only pay indirect taxes. They are different from other people in the group, since unlike them the others are able to create their own independent businesses and are large enough to avoid economic exploitation by the economic elites. On the other hand, this part of the group sells their products to established/big businesses but obtain payment for their products at a lot lower than the true price signals from market, hybrid or firm, otherwise. They are exploited by the economic elites, who sell the products they purchase from them at high prices, but pay very little to these informal sector workers. Institutional incentive system requires involving for example the local chamber of commerce to work towards reducing the transaction costs involved for this group, so that they are not only brought into the formal economy, so that their economic exploitation is stopped, but which also empowers them enough to resist/save themselves from the political elites' extraction initiatives.

Here, another manifestation of extractive institutions in term of the collusion of the political and economic elites (limelight/active actor group) is that tax system is kept moth-eaten and least implemented with SROs (Statutory Regulatory Orders)[6] rampantly used to provide safe heavens for not just the politico-economic elites, but also the 'invisible actor' group, in return for votes in elections and financial support in election campaigning.

Subsidy schemes, which also feature in IMF programmes generally, are used as targeted initiatives to safeguard the vulnerable sections of the economy. The elitist setup in Pakistan, once again distracts correct targeting of these subsidies in favour of those who help them come in power (through votes and finances), no matter even if these collaborators do not qualify for a subsidy programme.

It will not be wrong to say that a certain feature is kept in the makeup of the extractive institutions by the elites, whereby vulnerabilities could be created and exploited, in terms of for example providing low quality education and health services to people so that they have little leg to stand and earn their income on their own. Rather, conditions such as these are created whereby they remain dependent on the elites. Some of these vulnerable remain outside the formal economy at the back of little education and skills, and act as small private militias of these elites. These may be called overall as the 'expendable actors' group, used primarily by the political elites, for example in the largest metropolitan city of the country, Karachi, to carry out extortion from small businessmen and people from the services sector, who after retaining a small amount, give the rest to these elites. It is sources of income like this that apart from widening the gap of income inequalities between the active- and docile actors, also enhances the ability of political elite to spend huge sums to bribe the poverty-stricken majority of the electorate to vote for them. It is reasons like these that have kept Pakistani political system more a plutocratic phenomena and less a democracy.

In rural settings, the feudal landlords (part of limelight/active actor group) have people belonging to the expendable actor group in high number. These people play a big role in helping the landlord keep the small farmer under suppression. Moreover these farmers/tenants are pressurized to work at low wages on the farms, and are stopped from raising voice for greater property rights in return for years of their work tilling lands. In the urban settings a part of this expendable group is also in the shape of low paid, low ranked police officers, while in the rural areas along with the police, there is a section of poor semi-literate religious leaders (in the sense of small local setting) who also form a part of this expendable group. Both the police and religious leaders (in general at that level) assist the elite landlord in extracting from the local population through suppression caused by misuse of formal police power, and through these religious leaders who place informal writ on uneducated poor village people/small farmers by wrongly applying/interpreting religious laws in the

---

[6] SROs are special instructions from the Federal Board of Revenue (federal tax collection authority in Pakistan). These instructions/rules are in addition to the annual budget, are brought into effect without taking parliamentary approval, and are in principal for a limited time period.

matters of settling, for example inheritance, or keeping the female gender out of practical- and political life.

Yet another part of this expendable group is the low paid, local level revenue official (called a 'patwari' in the local sense; and present in both rural and urban areas), who specifically helps the elite by creating situations (by wrongly applying administrative rules, for example) through which both the docile- and the out of favour invisible actors are deprived of their private landed property. The power of political elites at their back has served as a great motivation for expendable actors, and has allowed them to survive for a long time. These loyalist actors also do electioneering for the elites, pursuing and forcing people to vote for these elites.

Sizeable representation of lower level judiciary (once again a low paid and a vulnerable group) also remains a part of this expendable group, who intentionally (at the back of bribes by elites) or unintentionally (with low pays acting as a disincentive) for example takes lukewarm action against weak and slow prosecution preparation by the police. An institutional matrix that provides positive and negative incentives to check the weak role played by judiciary to safeguard the docile actor (mainly), and which builts-in against the creation of huge back log of judicial cases (especially related to revenue) is a must to dismantle the extractive institutional setup, created and perpetuated by the elites.

In the light of the above, it can be seen that these expendable- and invisible actors are a great cause for high transaction costs and information asymmetries, and who hurdle proper fulfillment of contracts and reduce the level of protection of property rights. They do this at the behest of elites, who keep the governance structures weak so that these actors continue in their work without much problem/interference. Manipulation and artificial conditions thus introduced in the economy means that market, hybrid and firm environments find it difficult to reduce transaction costs, induce learning and innovation (through lack of protection of property rights) and in turn impact negatively on recovering true price signals. Overall, this lowers stability and growth in the economy. IMF programmes in particular and policy overall in general, have at best been naive by just viewing the environment through the lens of NCE behavoiural assumptions, and not focusing on improving institutional quality that could meaningfully deter the elites and their supporting actors.

In such an environment it is important that IMF programme conditionalities put focus on improving political- and economic institutions so that the size of the economy is enlarged and augmented by bringing the 'invisible actor' group into the formal economy, along with the 'limelight/active actor' group also put under formal institutional constraints, so that tax base is enhanced and the overall extractive institutional system could be dismantled.

It may also be pointed out here that it is this action matrix of actors (and which has built up from its rudimentary form since colonial times) that has left a strong influence on the evolution of informal- and formal institutions; has resulted in the creation of a value system that does not do justice in terms of properly reflecting the message of the underlying belief system. Hence, a misrepresented value system has produced sub-optimal behaviours and conventions, and ultimately law and governance structures. Policy (including the IMF programmes) has not been able to understand the problem in a wholesome way, which is why the scope of intervention is not at all context specific.

4.3.3 Challenging the Assumptions and Actions of Policy

Economic policy prescription in Pakistan, whether entirely home grown or negotiated under IMF programmes, has viewed the world from the lens of economic orthodoxy. Overall NCE assumptions have continued to make sense for policy thus far, while the ground realities were always more in line with a heterodox world-view generally, and NIE particularly.

NCE views the world as one where transactions entail no cost. In a world of imperfect information, the exchange economy works more and more in an impersonal way. In developing countries like Pakistan, where the state provides less support in lowering or meeting these costs, which include cost of searching a job, screening and selecting an employee, or securing one's private property among others, these costs were high to start with and have continued to rise. More importantly, transaction costs feed into the production costs of individuals, in turn reducing competitiveness and overall level of investment and economic growth.

Looking through the lens of thought process of NIE, *four* important aspects remained overlooked in Pakistan: (a) the role of transaction costs and needed institutional focus (b) the nature of incentive system that continued to shape the institutional system with attributes that supported extraction, (c) the relation between institutions and organizations, and (d) the interaction between formal and informal institutions, and how the link remained weak in terms of improving the short-comings of each other.

(a) **Transaction costs and institutions** NCE has thought of the production function of the economy to be composed of capital and labour, and simultaneously, therefore, the costs are only the ones that are linked with sustaining the structures of these two production factors. Hence, financial institutions from which capital is accumulated and distributed, and firms which are composed of managerial staff, workers and the related technology, have remained the focus of policy. This orthodox view of policy has not been able to realize the importance of transaction costs, and neglected the role of institutions that could have otherwise helped in reducing such costs.

In the presence of high transaction costs, market structure remained difficult for young firms to remain competitive in, and compete with producers enjoying economies of scale. This environment of imperfect competition resulted in creation of oligopolies and monopolies in various sectors, and hence brought about price signals that were much higher than to be produced from a perfectly competitive setting. This situation resulted in inflationary pressures. At the same time high transaction costs meant lowering of profits, which served as a disincentive to produce. Another disincentive to produce (less aggregate supply (AS)) came in the shape of lower aggregate demand (AD) at the back of built-up of inflationary pressures. All of this set in a spiral like situation, whereby less AD, resulting in less AS, reduced the demand of labour force as compared to the number of people willing and able to work, resulting in wages settling at a low level. Lower wages than before reduced purchasing power of employed labour, and together with higher unemployment rate resulted in lower AD, which in turn meant that output equilibrium stood settled at a lot lower level than it should have been had AS and AD stood at their potential levels. Hence, except from windfall gains in the shape of international commodity prices of imports falling or exports increasing, or through large injections of foreign loans, the growth rate remained stuck at sub-optimal production/output equilibrium levels.

In heterodox literature, an economy is basically viewed in terms of exchanges that take place between buyers and sellers in the setting of a market, a firm, or a hybrid. Moreover, NIE points out that a particular setting is selected where the transaction costs got minimized for that sector. It also means, at the same time, that while true price signals result where the allocation of resources is Pareto optimal, yet reaching such optimality is not possible without minimizing the transaction costs involved. Transaction costs in Pakistan are high for many reasons, and will be explained below.

The main reason for high transaction costs in Pakistan is a lack of protection of property rights. From publishing a book to creating an audio record, to owning a piece of land, performance of formal institutions has remained below expectations in terms of safeguarding the rights of the people to own, to feel secured for their property, or to transfer it easily. Political- and economic elites have been a major source of preferentially employing governance structures to safeguard their own property, to create situations/pressures whereby the owner of the property is either forced to leave his property rights in favour of these elites at a lower than market price, or the elite simply succeeds in usurping someone else's property and shows it as his own in official documents.

This selective use of governance structures to keep alive the extractive institutional setup creates a disincentive to innovation. The reason is that people have to spend a substantial amount of their profits from the employment or existence of their property (for example in the shape of earnings from produce of agricultural land, royalties on books, or revenue from sale of medicine) to safeguard their property rights from being snatched (piece of agricultural land getting occupied, for instance, or for example someone else's book published as one's own). All these costs enter into production costs, as transaction costs. The spectrum of these costs is large, ranging from entering into litigation, to start with. Lower judiciary in Pakistan suffers from a huge back log of cases, especially the revenue/land related cases. Here, once again the lack of will on the part of lower judiciary is more a case of 'manufacture' by the elite than an outcome of lack of financial resources to deal properly and appropriately quickly with the cases, which in turn results in the creation of huge back log of cases. The underlying purpose of this intervention by the political elite has been to keep alive the collusion with the economic elites for conducting extraction through usurping other's property rights.

Secondly, the moth-eaten and lackluster effort/performance of formal institutions like police and anti-corruption outfits means that many sufferers of property rights violations use either their 'contacts' in the shape of elites or their second-in-command accomplices (for example invisible actors), to move these outfits/formal institutions to take action against the other group of elites. Nothing comes cheap as another transaction cost in the shape of financial corruption kicks in, either in terms of pushing contacts to activate the formal institutions, or in other cases to bribe them directly. The formal institutions should have otherwise provided these safeguards, since they have been created and sustained through tax money of citizens to perform this function.

This relevance of contacts also creates a disincentive to getting true public representation in parliament. In exchange of providing these services, these contacts or a particular political elite group(s) binds people into being dependent on them rather than the state. Under the social contract, people gave up a part of their freedom by allowing creation of a state and within it constraints of informal- and formal institutions, so that through a deserving public leadership their rights (including property rights) could be protected. Moreover, an environment fostering minimal transaction costs in turn for innovation would be created, learning and economic growth to kick in, so that people overall could free themselves from their survival and growth worries. Yet this reliance on 'contact(s)' has been doing just the opposite, whereby the social contract is weakening in the face of politico-economic elite collusion becoming more reliable and dependable for the people to go to, than the informal- and formal institutions. Such a reliance and dependence has come at a big cost, and that is undeserving people (or political elites) getting into power rather than people who stand up for inclusive institutions.

This elitist group has continued to expand in Pakistan, raising the level of extraction and also transaction costs, and in turn has also been a major source of increasing income inequality. Such costs take away from profits of a sole owner or his shareholders, and also leave little room for reinvestments for further innovation and learning, with negative consequences in terms of slow growth in research and development, in improvement of human capital, on standard of living and overall economic growth.

(b) **Incentive system and extractive institutions** Institutions are the constraints that the society takes upon itself to reach productive and allocative efficiencies. The informal institutions are the basis for formal institutions. The values, norms and conventions of a society, in turn, are coded into implementable laws. Hence, laws or formal institutions provide the environment or the rules of the game, under which organizations that are the players of the game (under these rules) will act/behave. Institutions built this environment through an 'institutional matrix' that defines the 'incentive system', which in turn could be in the shape of 'negative incentives' or punishments, and 'positive incentives' or rewards. It is this nature of incentive system that basically defines the difference between underdeveloped and developed countries, since in the former the institutional matrix incentivizes inclusive behaviour in organizations, and in the later extractive behaviour.

Before independence the colonial rule evolved an incentive system that created local elites. The colonials gave them inordinate share in that initial distribution of agricultural land to make them economic elites, which in turn served as wealth needed to run political campaigns and contest elections, making them the indigenous political elite. These elites in the independent country continued with the same institutional matrix, as in colonial times; features of which are being alluded to here.

Instead of rewarding investments (a positive incentive) in human- and technological built-up that focused on innovation and learning, political elites legislated (or in other words provided formal institutions) in a way that the economic elites (and supporting economic actors, as discussed earlier) in markets and firms who supported political elites in extracting resources from the many in the economy (for example, treasury through annual budgets or SROs, gave special tax privileges or subsidies, or financial institutions providing easy and inordinate loan access, which was many a times also written-off through cooked up technical reasons) were allowed to have undue market power. Hence, this kind of extractive institutions did not provide a competitive environment for markets and firms, whereby economic elites invested their energies in coming up with plans to favour political elites and in turn were not checked for anti-competitive behaviour like forming cartels or for charging unfair prices. Hence, the unjustified profits they reaped as a consequence of this free ride provided them with enough fiscal space as not to allow transaction costs feed into final production costs. This situation helped in charging a far lower price than the 'small fish' that were not the economic elites and hence had to exit the market- or firm space. They simply could not compete with economic elites in such an environment. This extraction has led to many negative consequences.

Lack of check through the incentive matrix on this anti-competitive behaviour while made these economic (and in turn political) elites to become rich, but the unemployment this caused as a consequence, resulted in negative impact on stability and growth, along with enhancing income inequality and poverty. At the same time, lack of competition at home resulted in low levels of investment in innovation, making in turn Pakistani exports losing space in international markets to international competitors. This did not allow the country to enhance the quantity and quality of its exports, which resulted in reaching perpetually low levels of reserves, keeping in turn alive, the constant need for IMF resources to avoid BOP crisis. At the same time, easy and frequent access of IMF resources, even at the back of low programme implementation rate since the late 1980s, appears to be a strong reason for the country becoming a prolonged user.

Cartelization also meant that lack of competition and low investments in learning (to improve the quality of labour and technology) led to productive and allocative inefficiencies, and eventually to a higher market price than would have been under a competitive environment. Hence, this resulted in more inflation than should have been. The backing of the political elites also meant a soft corner by the competition regulator towards the excesses of cartels, who arbitrarily released products in markets to artificially keep the prices high through causing demand pull inflation.

This in turn raises questions on the independence of regulators. The political elites in Pakistan have not allowed regulators, checking competition in markets and firms, and working in sectors from commodity to energy to financial spheres, to remain out of the control of the executive. This is how the executive (mostly a product of political elites) have continued to meet their own economic- and political shortcomings in terms of performance, and also safeguarded the collaborating economic elites from the checks/punishments (negative incentives) of regulators, by influencing organizations/regulators through the extractive institutional setup. For example, central bank itself through printing money in excess of what it should have (causing inflationary pressures as a consequence), or commercial banks themselves (in attraction of getting higher interest rates on loans from government than would have otherwise from private sector) or under the influence of central bank provided a lot of access of deposit money to the executive (leaving little to meet the private sector liquidity needs for investment) came to the rescue of the political elites.

Institutional matrix, it can be seen therefore, has been used to meet vested interests. In this way, having a policy framework influenced by economic orthodoxy, in IMF programmes and otherwise, has produced a disconnect between ground realities and policy prescription. Foremost, economic growth has felt the negative consequence of this disconnect, since the institutional matrix has been creating inefficiencies in the economy by assuming that the 'invisible hand' of the market will fix them with least intervention of the government, which has been primarily seen to crowd out the private sector. Here, again the vested interests influencing institutional matrix to extract resources has meant that the political elite based executive and supported by economic elites, have been creating governance structures that crowded out 'on purpose', rather than such a thing coming about as a natural consequence of governments being bad for economic growth if they exist beyond the most minimum.

This once again is a NCE assumption that ill suits the heterodox thinking, which sees a necessary role of government to create an environment to crowd in the private sector. This feels a natural prescription for developing countries like Pakistan where corrected institutional matrix is required to reduce the burden of transaction costs, which originate because individuals or groups are not safeguarded through the invisible hand or lopsided actions of regulators in terms of contract enforcement and private property rights protection. This correction needs to bring an institutional incentive system that creates governance structures whereby investing in improving education and health services, competitiveness, and judicial writ is linked with receiving reward in terms of jobs, profits, less information asymmetries and reduced transaction costs, for the individuals, and giving of votes for true public representation.

IMF programmes (negotiated between country authorities and IMF staff), which have been based on Neo-Classical/Monetarist behavioural assumptions, saw little presence of these transaction costs, which as it can be seen feed into production costs, and hurt economic growth through various channels, including macroeconomic instability channel. Moreover, programme conditionalities show little recognition of the existence of elitist presence in the economy, and how these groups have constructed an incentive matrix that has perpetuated extractive institutions, maneuvering in turn formal institutions to selectively protect property rights and to use governance structures (under this formal institutional setup) to creating dependency of electorate on the elites, by keeping their growth educationally stunted and economically weak.

IMF programmes have not been able to support institutional reform that could obstruct and reform this extractive institutional matrix. Rather, it has suggested structural reforms, which only tries to manage the outcomes, created by this institutional matrix, while the architects of the institutional matrix (the political elites) continued to firmly retain themselves as executive, finding new ways (in connivance with economic elites) to continue with extraction. Structural reforms have just suggested changing the composition/share of individual economic sectors in the overall economy, but have not challenged the institutional matrix in favour of one that promotes inclusive institutions rather than extractive institutions.

In continuation with its inclination towards NCE, the recipe of structural reforms in the eyes of IMF programmes has remained to liberalize the economy and crowd out the government as far as possible through deregulation/privatization. Given the high level of transaction costs and continued perpetuation of influence of political- and economic elites over market outcomes, requires a context-specific focus on improving the quality of institutions, so that government crowds in the private sector through providing conducive environment (through a negative and positive incentive system) for optimal economic activity to take place, to enhance the level of efficiency by recovering optimal price signals and by protecting the vulnerable sectors through provision of well-targeted subsidies (for a rational time period only so they do not fall into the trap of infant-industry argument, as remained the case in Pakistan; and that these vulnerable sectors are enabled and pushed by policy towards self-sustainability).

Mere structural reforms will not work because at any given point of the state of the economy, the elitist institutional matrix will still control the economy enough to continue extraction. This one-size-fits-all kind of policy or structural reform practiced in IMF programmes in many regions of the world was not context-specific to developing countries in particular, as was evident in the experience of Latin America in the 1990s. Notwithstanding the limitations of structural reform as were adopted in IMF programmes, sustained positive consequence of economic growth requires institutional focus by the Fund. But before carrying out such a reform it is important to understand ground economic realities, in both its statics and dynamics, some of which are:

(i) Level and spread of transaction costs across the economy is high, and includes political- and economic domains, and actors.

(ii) Efficiency of transactions in terms of minimum transaction costs can be achieved through the governance structure of either a market, a firm, or a hybrid (Groenewegen et al. 2010), depending on the composition of a particular sector of the economy. NIE, unlike NCE, assumes that economic agents have bounded rationality, have vested interests and can behave in an opportunistic way. Hence, in contracting parties doing a transaction, if there is high dependency of one party on the other for completing the contract, then the other party can take advantage of this. In such a case it will not be possible to leave the matter to market forces alone, but governance structures will need to include administrative controls in the shape of checks on the hierarchy of a firm, or some kind of controls on market forces to avoid/stop from happening exploitation of one party by the other, and a combination of both kinds of checks in the case of a hybrid environment, so that optimal prices are reached at, and that transaction costs are kept at a minimum.

IMF programmes, under the influence of NCE thought process have not been context specific enough to acknowledge moral hazard and asset specificity[7] issues that remained high in Pakistan on account of opportunistic behaviour. Hence, IMF programmes (and policy in general) need to improve the governance structures of the market, firm and the hybrid so that the issues of price distortions, like commonly faced in Pakistan, do not hurt stability and growth performance.

Moreover, information asymmetries run the danger of a moral hazard issue when the agent has more information than the principal, and takes advantage of this situation in terms of maximizing his own welfare at the cost of the welfare of the principal (Groenewegen et al. 2010). In the case of Pakistan, the elites (the agent) have been delegated power as representatives of public (the principle) to take decisions which are Pareto optimal. Instead of creating governance structures that lower transaction costs in terms of information asymmetries for example, the contrary is pursued so that the agent enjoys the advantage of being the first to have information and has ready access to it, and in turn renders efficiency losses to the principal by making use information in a sub-optimal way (for example, by keeping it secret from general public).

(iii) Impersonal exchange dominates economic activity, which gives rise to bringing in safeguards through formal institutions that ensure that contracts are abided by. In the absence of such institutions or lack of governance structures to uphold these rules in Pakistan, there are high transaction costs faced by contracting parties in terms of putting in place personal/private mechanisms to lower the risk of contract violation. Absence of such protective governance

[7] As to how much an asset is relevant and needed for a particular kind of transaction, in terms of how much it will lose its value if it has to be put to use for another kind of transaction (Groenewegen et al. 2010, p. 369).

structures also increases the level of risk in the economy that negatively affects the level of economic activity, investment, and economic growth.

(iv) Property rights are seminal for economic growth, as they were for the progress of countries that now form the developed world. Low level of property rights protection results in little innovation, reduced competitiveness, lower investment and economic growth. The political elites in Pakistan through their power have been able to usurp and distribute property rights in their own favour (and their collaborators). This extraction has come at the cost of overall low levels of investment and economic growth in the economy, with increase in income inequality and poverty levels in Pakistan. Lack of protection of property rights from extractive institutions enhances the cost of doing business on one hand, and on the other hand leads to lower levels of innovation. This has resulted in competitiveness of Pakistani exports remaining low, and a major reason behind achieving low levels of export earnings, which remains one major influence for the existence of small build-up of foreign exchange reserves, the perpetual hovering of clouds of BOP crisis, and the incessant need for external borrowing.

(v) Institutional matrix is controlled by political- and economic elites, with roots of its formation in pre-colonial times, and contains incentive structure that promotes extractive institutions. Hence, structural change/reform focus is a limited approach by IMF, since merely changing the relative share of sectors in the economy will not be enough. To hold off the political- and economic elites from causing extraction requires by IMF to revise programme conditionalities that can transform the existing institutional matrix in favour of inclusive institutions.

(vi) Extractive institutional setup creates imperfect markets, safeguarding in turn the interests of the elites by evolving formal institutions that create flaws in governance structures that deal with regulation, so as to allow unfair benefit to the business interests of the political and economic elites. Such regulatory distortions and biased incentive structure have allowed undue market power and share in the hands of elites, who either have assumed monopoly powers or formed cartels in the process, in turn, gaining control over price setting. Commodity market is a prime example in this regard in Pakistan. Hence, IMF conditionalities need to understand the limitation of invisible hand policy prescription, and over emphasis on demand side of the economy to curtail inflation. This is because, left alone these market imperfections have distorted price signals, artificially creating inflationary pressures and affected stability in the short run, with negative consequences on output and employment in the long-run. Inability, of Fund programmes specifically and policy in general, over the years to broaden the focus to improving institutional quality has resulted in stagflationary consequences for the economy.

(c) **Relation between institutions and organizations** According to NIE while institutions are the rules of the game, organizations are the players of the game. Clear distinction was not understood or deliberately exploited in

Pakistan. The narrow policy of structural reform, under IMF programmes or otherwise, which focused on individual organizations and tried to bring change through within the governance structures of organizations, rather than impacting/creating institutions that could change the whole environment so that a different set of institutional incentive system could have pushed/evolved organizations in a different way. Changes through policy recommendations to deal with a certain outcome of a problem at the organizational level, with deeper roots in the environment, remained an impotent and unsustainable solution since it did not deal with the causes in the institutional matrix responsible for the problem. Rather than focusing on the political- and economic institutions, policy focused on political and economic organizations and that too in an opportunistic way to meet vested interests.

This rationality bounded approach resulted in sub-optimal consequences for the majority of population, at the cost of enabling extraction for the elites, resulting in increased income inequality gap and poverty levels. For instance, instead of an overall institutional matrix and within it an incentive system that evolves the governance structures of the entire economy, and the financing requirements and how to reach them, so that a single source chalks out an institutional framework while the organizations like the planning commission, finance ministry, departments related with labour and population management issues, follow the rules of the game, and improves them by providing a feedback to the overall economic institution; so that feedbacks of organizations are made sense of at one source, and institutional matrix is revised in a wholesome way.

Currently, organizations evolve their own institutional matrices and the governance structures accordingly, which lacks harmony of vision between different organizations, as more often than not the priorities and selection of economic objectives for the whole economy vary. Hence, while the planning commission plans a vision for the economy, the finance ministry and other ministries/departments may or may not be on the same page. This is because there is no one source working as an overall provider of institutional structure and incentive system, remaining in turn cognizant of the needs and feedback of all the players/organizations, and while that economic institution sets these organizations in motion with different objectives, but at the same time that institution ensures that all these organizations fulfill/move towards one wholesome policy vision for the entire economy.

Hence, one economic institution should have the power and responsibility to evolve the institutional matrix, taking feedback from organization in a continuous loop fashion. As a check, there may be some kind of independent evaluation setup (including an equal proportion of parliamentarians with economic expertise and private technocrats, to overall check the influence of elites, along with ensuring technical excellence) to keep a check on this institution, with some kind of voting system evolved to change/amend its decisions.

(d) **Formal and informal institutions** The value system originates from the belief system of a society, which in turn evolves the social conventions, and together these values and conventions form the informal institutions. Historically speaking, the area that now forms Pakistan, has remained under foreign occupations, especially since the medieval times, which although did bring unity to the otherwise warring small kingdoms, evolved the mental constructs of its population in a way that the value system remained more a reflection of that part of belief system that dealt with moral injunctions, and not of those parts that asked for educating oneself and to think on the lines of learning and innovation.

At no time in history due emphasis was placed on educating people. Hence, no such educationally invigorating environment came about like the one seen in Baghdad or Cordova in the medieval times, and later on during the Renaissance period. Therefore, the social mental constructs that Pakistan received through its citizens were overall tribal and primitive in their orientation. This primitive nature of people, preserved and perpetuated further by the extractive nature of colonial experience, meant that people themselves became used to 'serving' rather than 'struggling' for creating space to think freely, and securing property rights in a way that enabled them to innovate.

Given this background of the rulers and the ruled, roots of democracy remained weak on account of not meeting its pre-requisites. Rather, instead of democracy, plutocracy seems have been perpetuating itself. Masses with little education and little economic independence have not been able to produce a leadership or support it adequately when it did come about, in a way that the forces of status quo/elites could be checked properly. On the other hand, it appears that the elite's extractive ways and control of power to keep people uneducated to the extent that they either feel too weak or are not even inclined to struggle for evolving mental constructs that allows them to take from that part of their belief system that pushes for learning and innovation in all fields of life, seems to have been out powering the anti-status quo initiatives of the minority (who did receive enough quality education to evolve their mental constructs appropriately enough to launch some kind of struggle).

The makeup of informal institutions on these lines has meant that the formal institutions (coded rules) that have come about continue to lack the elements/substance that could put needed attention for evolving governance structures and arranging appropriate finances that result in placing necessary focus on education, reduction of transaction costs, and protection of property rights. The mental constructs that have come about through centuries of neglect and designed efforts by extractive institutional mentality, have resulted in producing an electorate that lacks the strength and vigour to push the representatives in parliament to implement needed reform. Rather the focus of the electorate has been reduced since long to a role whereby overall they continue to reconfirm their allegiance to the elites in return for assistance in meeting day-to-day economic- and community-level conflict resolution concerns.

It is here that the IMF programme conditionalities need to focus on, in terms of pushing investments in education, in reduction of transaction costs, and in protection of property rights so that people can reach/evolve those mental constructs that enable them to fully understand the immense importance and advantages of learning and innovation for (macroeconomic stability and) economic growth, and proper distribution of national income through availability of greater opportunities in the shape of inclusive institutions.

Policy overall will have to understand that institutions, extractive or inclusive, and formal or informal, are a product of a 'footpath' phenomena (Hayek 1979). It means that institutions evolve in a path dependent manner, and once developed as a consequence of path following that gets generated in the presence of extractive nature of elites, for instance, would require consistent policy to change the path direction. Effort, sustained over time, will be required both at the level of informal- and formal institutions to chalk out a new path in the shape of an incentive structure that transforms mental constructs to those that aspire and struggle for inclusive institutions, and that support learning and innovation. IMF programme conditionalities can make exogenous interventions to augment the process of this change in mental constructs by creating incentive structures, implementable through formal institutions. The incentive structures thus formulated will bring innovation and investment over time, reducing the risk of BOP crisis through enhanced level of exports, and will usher in sustained economic growth.

Moreover, informal- and formal institutions affect each other; on one hand, conventions becoming the basis of law, while on the other hand, the implementation of law feeds into mental constructs and through it into values and conventions. Hence, both evolve through this feedback loop. Although in Pakistan, the broad formal institutions have remained adherent of informal institutions, yet in terms of underlying governance structures, there is a big gulf created by the extractive institutional environment. At the same time, the extractive institutional environment has also not allowed necessary correction in informal institutions. It can be said then that broad postulates in the constitution or in formal institutions also need some revision so that such governance structures can be achieved at that put implementation of law on strong footing against the extractive institutional setup.

4.3.4 Designing an Institutional Incentive Structure for Pakistan

Acemoglu and Robinson (2006) indicate that power is difficult to take away, since political elites have the experience of attaining, exercising, and retaining power, as they most often than not are successful in going around the de jure formal institutions through bribing, lobbying, and simply coercion. Their collusion with economic elites gives them technical knowhow as how to for example evade taxes, and this collusion over time reaches an equilibrium extractive institutional setup through the use of an institutional matrix that has extractive incentive system. The same could be seen in Pakistan, where over time the so called '22 families' or a small elite group in the 1960s has ballooned, including representation from all organs of the state, and across income groups.

The hope lies in empowering the masses with an educational system that develops the mental constructs in ways that focuses their attention to reforming both the backwardness features of the informal institutions, and the aspects of impracticality, lack of necessary details, and an inbuilt implementation mechanism of the formal institutions, along with governance structures evolved through them. Overall with education at the heart of it all, there needs to be brought about an institutional change and through it an inclusive incentive system that stops extraction, brings power into the hands of that public representation that earns it through performance and not through coercion and bribery. Moreover, apart from the subjects related with national security and strategic assets/projects, everyday economy is run through an inclusive setup/arrangement between elected local governments and provincial/national parliamentarians, along with building up the judiciary, the bureaucracy, and the technocracy to ensure protection of contractual and property rights so that the cost of doing transactions is reduced to the minimum through the use of market, hybrid and firm governance structure. Lastly, a crowding in role of the government is brought in so that efficiency losses are reduced to the minimum.

Each of the above mentioned goals need an incentive system, that is both inclusive and that penetrates and causes two-way horizontal interaction between the informal and formal institutions, along with two-way vertical interaction between institutions and organization. It also needs to remain flexible to cover all the three governance structures of markets, firms and hybrids depending on a particular kind of transaction (in terms of actors involved, asset specificity, frequency of transaction, and uncertainty). Moreover, the system needs to internalize the different kinds of property rights (for example, rights related with landed property or intellectual property) and the specific needs for protecting each one of them.

The importance of data collection and its transparent dissemination is immense in the overall attainment of sustained level of stability and growth. In Pakistan a lot of work needs to go in this direction, and has to be high on the agenda items of institutional matrix. Improved data related aspects will play an important role in setting up efficient and more accountable organizational structures. Moreover, through an independent evaluation oversight/setup, data is kept safe from the vested interest attacks/manipulation of the elites.

Let's analyze in detail some of the major aspects of an institutional incentive system:

(i) **Education** Institutional change starts with a training of the mind to think with clarity and understanding in an objective way. Symbol of unity of federation is the state, and through it, the federal government. Being a republic, it is the responsibility of public representatives to legislate formal institutions that educate its citizens so that they can fulfill their potential as electorate, as proper custodians of family life, and as the brains capable of understanding religion and follow properly its injunction from ethics to exploring the world to understand the nature of things and affairs for bringing/enhancing welfare of mankind.

That is a wholesome agenda, and requires a syllabus at the school, college and university levels, respectively, that can prepare the minds accordingly. It also requires a pool of teachers who are qualified to teach. It requires uniformity of purpose and instruction so that every child is provided with an equal opportunity to excel, retaining a balance between individualistic aspirations and nationalism. The medium of instruction needs to be English for those subjects where knowledge, like sciences, social sciences, western philosophy, and mathematics, is best delivered through it. Side by side, on equal footings teaching Urdu (national language) for subjects that empower people to communicate properly and fluently in their national life, and which enables people to understand the view point of philosophers, and historians mainly of the East.

Moreover, informal educational programmes are also needed to be launched to improve the level of literacy among those segments of society that have otherwise passed the age of joining the formal educational streams.

Being a federation, the units have a right to preserve regional outlook and philosophy to the extent that it does not hinder the goals at the national level, for which the units joined in to form one country. For this, regional languages should be taught, and depending on each province's (or a federating unit's) preference as reflected through its particular parliament, main regional language is taught as a compulsory or as an optional subject. Overall, the reform in educational institutional matrix should be equally applicable for both genders (male and female that is).

From above, it is clearly the responsibility of the public sector to create the environment and structures that enable education of people, on the lines broadly indicated above. It should also remain welcoming for the private sector to join in, only if it can meet the institutional requirements and incentive system set by the government/public sector. Financing estimates of required expenditure/investment needs of the educational sector to be clearly reached at for the whole country by the central government, and that too as quickly as possible through domestic resource mobilization and harmonized/properly targeted utilization of foreign assistance (from development partners/donors).

The structure needs to have clarity in terms of hierarchy, simplicity through minimum personnel and no disguised labour (no extra support staff that is). Also, it has to be well defined, humane and having modern standards for the employers and employees in the sector (like time limit for keeping a staff as contractual) in terms of rights and duties. Moreover, the selection process needs to have a well designed examination system, and should be transparent, objective and merit based.

These are roughly the overall building blocks of the incentive system of the institutional matrix for education. The implementation mechanism needs regulatory check/oversight of the education authorities, and has to be empowered to take adequate action against violators (through negative incentive or punishment). In the spirit of its importance, education related action taken by the regulatory authorities should be adequately supported by law enforcement agencies (police and its investigative branch), and by pro-active and impartial judicial process that also avoids creation of back log of cases.

Research organizations need to be evolved at every level of educational establishments, and a sound link created with industry, data collection authorities, and job market bureaus. A defining principle needs to be in the shape of inbuilt mechanisms whereby discretion by bureaucracy is strongly checked and no out of turn/merit postings/transfers allowed. Staff promotions should be linked with well defined multi-criteria benchmarks, and are fast-paced; while salaries and pensions are made market based, and technocrats are given most positions in the functioning and regulation of the sector, so that overall both the needed capacity and motivation levels built-up, and also independence of regulation ensured. Moreover, the size of the sector needs to be kept well-proportioned, so that there is no unnecessary fiscal burden, and any disguised labour that may exist gets pulled out, trained appropriately and employed productively in some other sector.

Every municipality provided with big libraries, since without access to ample and varied knowledge there can be no positive impact on mental constructs. All initiatives should be across rural- and urban centres, and all municipalities are brought to equal standing and footing in as short a time as possible, while all municipalities are built-up to meet the goals set under the institutional matrix. One of the initiatives to ensure smooth and timely flow of finance could be to map the educational financial requirements with taxes collected at a particular municipality level, while the difference is made up through other means and sources of financing.

Transaction costs need to be reduced in the education sector. Tuition system needs to be strongly checked so that teachers teach properly in their jobs, and students don't face extra educational costs (for getting guidance from teachers through their independent teaching setup, and not through the educational establishment where the teachers were legally obligated (since they formally work there) to impart education). For this positive incentives are important as well, whereby teachers are also paid competitive salaries, given fast track promotions on account of their classroom- and research performance. Transaction costs are also reduced by lowering search and information costs, for example, for new job vacancies or research funding opportunities, among others, in the education sector. Another positive incentive could be to link the addition in the amount of pension beyond a certain minimum that is, to the performance on above mentioned (and other similar) criteria. Also, an active teacher training process is initiated at all levels of education, and at all stages of teacher's career. A negative incentive should come in the shape of warnings, and even suspensions in the case of violation of rules. Moreover, research related travel and other costs are also supported, which will positively incentivize effort. At the same time, financial institutions and insurance companies need to be involved/engaged more actively to develop products for supporting employees and students in their educational endeavours.

Information asymmetries are high in developing countries in particular, so it is important to find screening procedures for selecting employees that work in the context of local conditions. Active research cells need to be created in this regard. Moreover, to answer the questions like which educational establishment qualifies for subsidies, or which among them meets other financial support requirements, models need to be evolved so as to avoid wrong award of these to those who become successful in obtaining this kind of support through fraud.

Property rights protection, for example for writers of their books, or other intellectual property rights, is extremely important, since it encourages learning and innovation. Moreover, strong negative incentive systems are built into the education reform package, whereby strict action is taken against violators by law enforcement agencies and judiciary.

The big question then is how to bypass the powerful politico-economic power base to make happen and sustain this intervention? An initiative will have to be launched from the platform of anti-status quo political party (or parties), and needs to take strength from all the like-minded civil society spheres, including that from the teacher fraternity is expected to add a lot of impetus. The struggle will need a lot of muscle in terms of will power. Yet as the movement starts to put pressure on the status quo and pushes for reform, even small changes in the existing system and the positive impact of these on mental constructs, will in time (depending on the speed of implementation of the institutional matrix) have a cascading effect. As it is, the path dependent nature of institutional change will mean that once the mental constructs adopt a more positive understanding of the importance of education, and through it see empowerment, the more resilience and momentum the movement will attain, making it in turn all the more difficult for the status quo to stop such a change from happening, and will not be able to survive in the process. This positive change will lead to better public representation and brighter chances for taking the educational reform further.

(ii) **Institutions for bringing inclusion** Governance structures should not be alien to ground realities, and for this it is important that local governments are seen as the core element of working for change. This means that the provincial and federal parliamentarians should legislate, in a way that they give utmost importance to the needs of the people at the municipality/local level. This is how grass roots level public representation will feel included in provincial and national level policy decisions. This is how true empowerment will be bestowed to the people.

(iii) **Strengthening the democratic system** Pre-requisites of democracy have remained weak at the back of primarily low educational level and lack of economic empowerment of the people. This has been both a result of backward nature of informal institutions overall, along with efforts put in by firstly the colonial legacy and then the perpetuation of this policy by the elite after independence, have kept the institutions extractive in nature. Hence, while the elites overtly talk about strengthening the roots of democracy in the country, covertly they have been strengthening the system of plutocracy. The way out is that as educational system gets reformed, resulting in mental constructs of people to improve in a way that they start to struggle with greater focus and motivation to become a more empowered citizenry, then the freedoms that will usher in, will bring true public representation on the basis of performance, while those who not deliver on needed reforms will be thrown out through elections.

(iv) **Role of elected local governments and provincial/national parliamentarians** Local self governance has to be the model that will bring sustained progress, and which will also be able to dilute the impact of political elites (see details in Sect. 4.3.5).

(v) **Build up of the judiciary, the bureaucracy, and the technocracy** Implementation of the institutional matrix requires sound governance structures. The role of judiciary, bureaucracy, and technocrats (field experts) in efficient working of the governance structures (in markets, hybrids, and firms) cannot be less emphasized, and therefore need to be augmented through evolving and implementing a meaningful incentive system.

(vi) **Defining a crowding in role of the government** High transaction costs, especially in terms of costs related with searching and screening, for meeting contractual obligations, and for securing property rights protection, serve as a disincentive or crowds out the private sector. Since transaction costs feed into overall production costs, and therefore impact macroeconomic stability and economic growth, therefore it is important that the institutional matrix defines a crowding in role of the government, so that the government evolves governance structures that reduces transaction costs to as minimum as possible, so that such costs are not faced by the private sector. This will create an attractive environment for the private sector and will induce greater learning, innovation and investment in the economy, in turn impacting positively on overall stability and growth.

4.3.5 Towards Optimal Governance Structures

The above mentioned goals need sequencing and structure. One model is suggested below as a starting point of further deliberation by policy (of IMF programmes and/or otherwise).

The economy is seen in terms of municipalities; hence being the lowest geographical denominator on the economic landscape. The role of the overall economic institution and the organizations under it (including the chambers of commerce), is to improve the economic conditions of the municipalities in line with this overall institutional matrix.

The overall spirit should be to use the resources of each municipality on itself, while the difference between current expenditures and where it ought to be to meet the overall institutional requirements, should be provided by evolving some constitutionally backed formula of resource sharing at the federal level. Care needs to be taken here and transparent and practical benchmarks need to be evolved so that lagging municipalities do not fall into a moral hazard issue, being unduly pampered at the back of some elitist intervention to meet his own vested interests.

The very reason for working at the municipality level is to break down the area of influence of the collusion of politico-economic elites to a reasonably smallest possible existence/sphere, so that any misuse of power can be unearthed and checked easily through restraining the scope of focus to the micro level. Working at the municipality level will also help lower the involvement of money in elections as well (a positive initiative in turn to cause a move from plutocracy to democracy) since the area of constituency will be small.

Moreover, municipalities will be empowered through ensuring their stronger say/role in policy making, by giving them adequate authority to work with provincial/federal parliamentarians. Also, the division of power made whereby local governments (at the municipality level) carry out development work with the help of technocrats, while parliamentarian at the higher level only legislate to provide overall adequate environment for economic activity to take place. Apart from bringing in economic gains, this initiative will also help distribute people standing for elections more appropriately, who will be clearly self selecting themselves into lawmakers or in running municipalities.

The overall institutional matrix and the governance structures should focus on mapping the expected taxes of each municipality and the expenditure needs, which match the quality and quantity requirements of the whole scope of reforms suggested in the institutional matrix and incentive system (including the current needs of running the economy of that particular municipality). As part of this effort, the importance of the role of markets, firms and their hybrid is also understood for each municipality, along with transaction costs and property rights issues also focused upon according to their specific presence in a particular municipality.

The incentive system evolved should ensure that the parliamentarians and the municipalities should work in an inclusive manner, on one hand. On the other hand, division of development effort at the municipality level and the restriction of parliamentarians to law-making will allow governance structures (law enforcement agencies, anti-corruption agencies, judiciary, and parliamentary oversight committees for example) to play their role more efficiently.

Administrative structures should also be laid out in a way that the hierarchy involves three layered structures: federal-, provincial- and municipal levels. Hence, each layer has an equal say or input weight in matters like carrying out administrative transfers/postings, so that the influence of hierarchy to throw its weight in a wrong way at the behest of an elitist intervention is made as difficult as possible. Parliamentary oversight committees are also formed, which keep a check on any delaying tactics of parliamentarians in bringing legislation necessary for the development work of the municipalities. Moreover, targets benchmarking for municipalities is linked with initial level of development of a municipality, and in turn making groups of similar municipalities, so as to make targets for each bracket of municipalities commensurate with their existing level and where they should be. This would bring practicality and fairness to the judgment process. Municipalities, which are either on track for meeting goals set under the institutional matrix or have met goals them in time, should be rewarded/provided positive incentives. Hence, better performing municipality rewarded, for example, in terms of better pays for the elected representatives of that municipality, and some monetary reward for the organs of the state and the private sector.

Judicial oversight is also made available to check any excesses of power by the administration and public representation in an efficient way through evolving the scope and capacity of judiciary. To augment the working of the spirit of separation of powers, and checks and balance elements for the organs of the state, the appeal system and activism in judicial discourse are structured to take their course in an efficient time and monetary frameworks. Rational incentive structures need to be evolved to keep the administration properly supported to perform its functions diligently while in service, and should feel well hedged after retirement in terms of competitive pensions/other benefits.

It may be pointed here that the current effort here to contextualize the institutional problem from the perspective of heterodox/NIE perspective is a novelty for Pakistan. In that sense, it is hoped that the placing of institutional analysis in a formal framework that is linked to ground realities, will help policy practitioners of the country and at IMF in revising their policy programmes.

4.4 Data and Methodology

4.4.1 Theoretical Design

Powerful elites (both political- and economic elites) take advantage of the overall weak institutional setup, and in turn are able to overcome checks placed through macroeconomic policies in one way or the other. In doing so they are able to extract resources and in turn become a source of macroeconomic instability, while traditional macroeconomic variables (targeted by policy) are only symptoms of the deeper institutional problem (Acemoglu et al. 2003). At the same time, weak institutional setup may also lead to coups, as was seen on many occasions in Pakistan (Acemoglu and Robinson 2001).

IMF programmes based on traditional Neo-Classical/Monetarist assumptions have not put attention to institutional determinants that can help check this opportunistic behaviour. Consequently, political- and economic elites in prolonged users like Pakistan have been able to take advantage of the weak institutional environment and extract resources (Hussain 1999; Khawaja and Khan 2009, p. 18). Moreover, over-emphasis of Fund programmes on traditional macroeconomic variables mostly, and not much on the institutional determinants, have not strengthened the needed institutional environment, whereby macroeconomic variables can effectively impact macroeconomic consequences. At the same time, inadequate institutional setup does not boost supply side factors, including business and investment environment that negatively impacts economic growth. Also, Haghighi et al. (2012), in a case study conducted on Iran, pointed out that there existed a long-term relation between economic growth and macroeconomic instability, and from Chap. 3 it could be seen that an increase in macroeconomic instability negatively impacts economic growth.

Given this background, in the current study, it is proposed that improvement in KOF Index of Globalization will result in a positive impact on macroeconomic stability (in other words, reducing macroeconomic instability) and real economic growth. An additional proposition will be that decrease in macroeconomic instability will also enhance real economic growth. The underlying proposition will be that macroeconomic instability will depend on institutional environment as well (and not just macroeconomic variables), since it will also be reduced by the improvement in determinants of institutional quality (in the current case being KOF Index of Globalization).

Based on the relationship between institutional quality (in terms of significant institutional determinants), macroeconomic instability and economic growth, established in the last chapter, this chapter aims at estimating the effect of improvement in institutional quality on macroeconomic instability and economic growth. More specifically, counterfactual analysis will be carried out to estimate the effects of determinants of institutional quality on MII, and on the average growth rate of GDP of Pakistan. For the analysis, however, continuous data is required; therefore I have focused only on KOF Index of Globalization as a determinant of institutional quality. The following discussion, therefore, focuses on the theoretical linkages of globalization on the sub-indices of macroeconomic instability, and hence on economic growth.

The first sub index of macroeconomic instability is the inflation rate. Inflation rate escalates instability through its effect on economic decisions regarding money demand, savings, and investment, which in turn harm economic growth. KOF Index of Globalization is an indicator of globalization. The economic dimension of globalization affects inflation rate through trade which is the main cause of purchasing power parity. Less restricted trade not only controls average inflation rate, it also minimize variability of the inflation rate.

Globalization has two competing effects on exchange rate variability. On the one hand, globalization makes a country more vulnerable to foreign shocks, thereby making exchange rate more volatile. On the other hand, more globalized economy can potentially earn more foreign exchange, accumulation of which saves domestic currency from speculative attacks. So exchange rate remains stable. Furthermore, both stable prices and exchange rate stability lead to stable real effective exchange rate.

The fundamental requirement of achieving higher growth rate is the enabling environment in which economic decisions are taken. If there is uncertainty regarding future inflation rate or exchange rate, then businesses cannot take optimal decisions regarding investment, saving and international trade. The sub-optimality of economic decisions discourages improvement in living standard of the citizens. Therefore, reducing macroeconomic instability is of utmost importance for achieving higher growth rate.

4.4.2 Sample

Time series data on Pakistan is taken for the duration 1980–2014 (since, during this time, Pakistan frequently used IMF resources). The data has been enhanced from 2009 (in the rest of book) to 2014, to avoid the degrees of freedom issue while applying the VAR (Vector Autoregression) approach.

4.4.3 Data and Variable Description

From Chap. 2, significant determinants of political- and economic institutional quality were estimated for IMF programme countries. In order to carry out Structural VAR (SVAR) analysis it is important to have variables that are neither qualitative, along with covering adequate time duration (for avoiding degrees of freedom issue). KOF index of globalization (or simply, 'KOF') has therefore been taken and its impact is being seen on MII (Macroeconomic Instability Index) and real economic growth.

Data on real GDP (RGDP) is taken from the World Economic Outlook (WEO) of the IMF.[8]

Based on the methodology and definitions of Ismihan (2003), Macroeconomic Instability Index (MII)[9] has been constructed using the following five[10] indicators:

(i) Inflation rate (INF; calculated by taking data on average consumer prices from WEO[11]),
(ii) Fiscal deficit (FD) as percentage of GDP.[12]
(iii) Public debt (PD; domestic debt plus external debt and liabilities) as percentage of GDP.[13]
(iv) Exchange rate variability (ERV) has been calculated on the basis of 12 month end-of-period nominal exchange rate in SDR, taken from IFS (IMF)[14] and,

[8] https://www.imf.org/external/pubs/ft/weo/2015/01/weodata/download.aspx

[9] For details, see Ismihan (2003, pp. 214–215), who constructed MII.

[10] It may be indicated here that while Ismihan (2003) only included the first four indicators to construct the MII, the current study augments it with one more indicator.

[11] https://www.imf.org/external/pubs/ft/weo/2015/01/weodata/download.aspx

[12] Data source is State Bank of Pakistan (http://www.sbp.org.pk/) and Ministry of Finance, Government of Pakistan (http://finance.gov.pk/survey_1314.html). Also, data on fiscal deficit is taken instead of budget deficit due to availability of data in this format for Pakistan.

[13] Data source is State (or central) Bank of Pakistan (SBP; http://www.sbp.org.pk/).

[14] Data taken from IFS CD ROM (IMF).

(v) Real Effective Exchange Rate Index (REER; taken from WDI[15] of the World Bank). This indicator has been included in Ismihan (2003) to augment MII to include the impact of competitiveness in it.

4.4.4 Econometric Methodology

The prime objective of this chapter is to conduct counterfactual analysis to see the effect of institutional quality on macroeconomic instability and real economic growth. For this purpose I have constructed a VAR using all sub-indices of MII and indices of institutional quality—KOF index of globalization.

Thereafter, appropriate restrictions are imposed on contemporaneous relationship of variables to make VAR identified, and to recover structural shocks. These shocks are then used to trace out the effect of KOF on sub-indices of MII, and real economic growth, respectively.

In the next step, counterfactual simulations are conducted, assuming a hypothetical situation in which IMF programme has an institutional focus. More specifically, the following three scenarios are assumed, with respect to improvement in institutional quality and their effect will be simulated on MII and log of real GDP, respectively:

(a) low scenario: institutional determinants are enhanced by 5 %;
(b) moderate scenario: institutional determinants are enhanced by 10 %; and
(c) optimistic scenario: institutional determinants are enhanced by 15 %.

The reason for taking these particular values is to see how enhancement in institutional quality in small steps impacts MII and real economic growth.

This procedure gives us one-time simulated figures. However, to be confident I have also done stochastic simulation in which the procedure for finding counterfactual MII and economic growth rate, is repeated 10,000 times using bootstrap procedure, and then the characteristics of distribution of MII and real economic growth in each scenario is presented and explained.

The impact of MII is also seen on real economic growth. Hence, the impact of institutional determinants is seen both directly on MII and real economic growth, and also on real economic growth indirectly, by seeing how a reduction in MII impacts real economic growth.

The SVAR Approach VAR has been employed by numerous researchers since Sims (1980), as an alternative to the traditional simultaneous equations systems in which the difference between endogenous and exogenous variables is not only difficult to find, but also looking for appropriate instruments is virtually impossible. Moreover, interdependence among variables is analyzed through impulse response functions. However, some restrictions need to be put on structural parameters, and structural shocks need to be recovered before estimating impulse response functions.

[15] http://data.worldbank.org/data-catalog/world-development-indicator

There are three types of restrictions imposed on structural parameters, namely the Choleski decomposition approach, Sims-Bernanke approach, and Blanchard and Quah approach. For example, in Choleski decomposition method, the ordering of the variables is done so that the matrix of structural parameters is a lower triangular and residuals are orthogonalized across equations (Leamer 1985; Cooley and LeRoy 1985). At the same time, instead of relying on identifying structural parameters in triangular fashion, Sims (1986) and Bernanke (1986) highlighted the role of economic theory in identifying structural shocks. In this regard, the restrictions may not however be on contemporaneous relationships among variables, and identifying restrictions may render the system over-identified. Finally, Blanchard and Quah (1989) proposed identification strategy through economic theory by imposing long run restrictions of one variable on the other.

Whether or not variables in the VAR should be differenced, when they are non-stationary, is a long debated issue. In this regard, according to Sims et al. (1990) transforming VAR, if variables are non-stationary, into stationary cointegrated system is not necessary. But some econometricians like Garratt et al. (1998) warn against making variables stationary if they contain unit root. However, if there exists long run equilibrium relationship among variables, VAR in level can be used, even if variables in the system are non-stationary (Sims et al. 1990; Sims 1992). The essential requirement, however, is that residuals from VAR model should be free from autocorrelation and heteroskedasticity.

In the light of the discussion above, it appears pertinent to lay down below some of the technical details of the VAR model used in the current study.

Suppose the following dynamic structural equations explain the dynamics of an economy.[16]

$$BY_t = \gamma_0 + \sum_{i=1}^{p} \gamma_1^i Y_{t-i} + \sum_{i=1}^{p} \gamma_2^i Z_{t-i} + \varepsilon_t \tag{4.1}$$

Here, B is the matrix of structural parameters representing contemporaneous response coefficients, Y_t is a vector of variables, containing indices of MII, and indicators of IQ. Where, γ_0 is a vector of constants, γ_1^i represents matrices of endogenous variables, while γ_2^i represent coefficient matrices of exogenous variables. Moreover, ε_t represents vector of structural innovations, which are IID (independently and identically distributed).

[16] From Chap. 3, it can be seen that in IMF programme countries, determinants of institutional quality have an overall negative impact on MII. Moreover, Acemoglu et al. (2003) pointed out that the main reason behind macroeconomic instability and the varying levels of macroeconomic volatility among different countries were related more with institutional reasons than the traditionally identified macroeconomic determinants. Similarly, better budgetary institutions (which are important economic institutions) had a negatively significant impact on (budget) deficit (von Hagen 1991). Note: for details on VAR and SVARs, see Chap. 5, 'Multiequation time-series models' of Walter Enders (2015).

There are six variables in the VAR model: inflation rate (INF), exchange rate (ER),[17] real effective exchange rate (REER), public debt (PD) and fiscal deficit (FD). Here, both PD and FD are taken as ratios of GDP, while KOF index of globalization has been taken as a determinant of institutional quality. Pre-multiplying above equation by B^{-1} on both sides to convert the system into VAR in standard form or reduced form VAR.

$$Y_t = A_0 + \sum_{i=1}^{p} A_1^i Y_{t-i} + \sum_{i=1}^{p} A_2^i Z_{t-i} + e_t \tag{4.2}$$

where,

$$A_0 = B^{-1}\gamma_0 \tag{4.3}$$

$$A_1 = B^{-1}\gamma_1 \tag{4.4}$$

$$A_2 = B^{-1}\gamma_2 \tag{4.5}$$

$$e_t = B^{-1}\varepsilon_t \tag{4.6}$$

It is important to note that reduced form residuals are related with the underlying structural shocks according to the final equation:

$$E\left(e_t e_t^{'}\right) = E\left(B^{-1}\varepsilon_t\right)\left(B^{-1}\varepsilon_t\right)^{'} \tag{4.7}$$

A critical step in VAR analysis is selection of appropriate lag length, which is helpful in capturing true dynamics of the economy and in finding reliable results. Wrong specification of lag length results in unreliable estimates (Braun and Mittnik 1993). More lags quickly consume degrees of freedom while selecting too few lags result in autocorrelated residuals (Lütkepohl 1991). Moreover, as Hafer and Sheehan (1991) highlighted, forecast accuracy also depends on lag length. Two criteria that are frequently used in research studies are AIC (Akaike Information Criterion) and SIC (Schwarz Information Criterion). The idea behind these criteria is that more lags reduce residual sum of squares (RSS), but consume more degrees of freedom. Both criteria compare benefit of reduction in RSS with the loss of degrees of freedom. If adding an additional lag reduces RSS more than the loss of loss of degrees of freedom, then that lag must be included in the VAR. The best model is where the value of either of these criteria is minimum.

After estimation of VAR in standard form, a researcher is required to put restrictions on coefficients to recover structural parameters from estimated reduced form residuals. There are $n(n-1)/2$ number of restrictions that need to be imposed to have an exactly identified system.

[17] I have employed ER in VAR model, but simulation analysis is based on ERV.

The VAR model in Eq. (4.1) has moving average representation, which can be found by recursive substitution method. The vector moving average form is given as:

$$X_t = \sum_{i=0}^{\infty} \theta_i \varepsilon_{t-i} \tag{4.8}$$

where,

$$\theta = A^{-1}[I - \gamma_1]^{-1} \tag{4.9}$$

or

$$Y_t = \overline{\theta}\gamma + \overline{\theta}e_t \tag{4.10}$$

Where,

$$\overline{\theta} = [I - \gamma_1]^{-1} \tag{4.11}$$

Structural shocks can be recovered from Eq. (4.1) by using structural parameters, after restricting some of the parameters.

I have put the restriction that institutional quality is causally prior to all other variables in the VAR. This assumption is justified as institutional quality affects macroeconomic variables, but the contemporaneous relationship is not true for the other way round. Within the sub-indices of MII, exchange rate is assumed to be immediately affected by all variables, while fiscal indicators and inflation rate are adjusted in the last. Overall, these assumptions are consistent with exchange rate overshooting model (Dornbusch 1976), fiscal theory of exchange rate (Oge Guney 2007) and the assumption of price rigidity in the economy.

4.5 Estimation and Results[18]

4.5.1 *VAR and Impulse Response Functions of Sub-indices of MII and KOF Index of Globalization*

In the first step, pretesting of unit root in the variables is important. I have used Augmented Dickey-Fuller (ADF) procedure to test the presence of unit root. As expected, most of the variables are found to be unit root processes, as shown in Table 4.1. Inflation rate and exchange rate variability are only stationary at level;

[18] Here, EViews 8 has been employed for estimation purposes (http://www.eviews.com/EViews8/ev8whatsnew.html).

Table 4.1 Results of ADF test

	Level			First difference		
Variables	ADF	Critical values	Probability	ADF	Critical values	Probability
ER	2.968524	−3.699871	0.9999	−3.263094	−3.689194	0.0267
ERV	−5.692251	−3.639407	0.0000			
FD	−2.490783	−3.639407	0.1265	−7.795269	−3.646342	0.0000
INF	−3.210213	−3.646342	0.0283			
KOF	−0.802918	−3.639407	0.8055	−5.694326	−3.646326	0.0000
LRGDP	−2.853124	−3.646342	0.0619	−3.665772	−3.653730	0.0097
MII	−2.460716	−3.646342	0.1339	−8.503539	−3.653730	0.0000
PD	−2.756072	−3.646342	0.0757	−4.700672	−3.646342	0.0006
REER	−2.000458	−3.639407	0.2853	−5.624953	−3.646342	0.0000

Table 4.2 Results of Johansen cointegration test

Series: ER FD INF KOF PD REER				
Unrestricted cointegration rank test (Trace)				
Hypothesized no. of CE(s)**	Eigenvalue	Trace statistic	0.05 critical value	Probability
None*	0.910570	210.2054	103.8473	0.0000
At most 1*	0.754857	135.3621	76.97277	0.0000
At most 2*	0.677771	91.77874	54.07904	0.0000
At most 3*	0.577992	56.67147	35.19275	0.0001
At most 4*	0.424355	29.92679	20.26184	0.0017
At most 5*	0.338414	12.80659	9.164546	0.0098
Unrestricted cointegration rank test (maximum eigenvalue)				
Hypothesized no. of CE(s)**	Eigenvalue	Max-eigen statistic	0.05 critical value	Probability
None*	0.910570	74.84337	40.95680	0.0000
At most 1*	0.754857	43.58334	34.80587	0.0035
At most 2*	0.677771	35.10727	28.58808	0.0063
At most 3*	0.577992	26.74468	22.29962	0.0112
At most 4*	0.424355	17.12020	15.89210	0.0320
At most 5*	0.338414	12.80659	9.164546	0.0098

*Indicates 1 % level of significance
**Cointegrating equations (CE(s))

the reason being that both variables are first differences of non-stationary variables, namely the inflation rate and exchange rate, respectively. However, none of the variables contain two unit roots so that all variables are stationary at first difference.

When variables are non-stationary at level then they have long run trend or permanent component. In this case, if variables are cointegrated then the system of equations should be modeled as vector error correction model (VECM), otherwise the procedure of VAR in first difference has to be adopted for these variables. The procedure, therefore, is to test the hypothesis of cointegration among the variables. I have employed Johansen's methodology to test cointegration among variables that are to be combined in VAR model. In Table 4.2, both the Trace test and Maximum

Table 4.3 VAR lag order selection criteria

Endogenous variables: KOF INF PD FD REER ER			
Exogenous variables: C			
Sample: 1980 2014			
Included observations: 31			
Lag	LR	AIC	SIC
0	NA	38.47708	38.75462
1	280.0967*	29.12896	31.07178*
2	36.78682	29.40783	33.01593
3	48.89836	27.65555*	32.92892

Table 4.4 VAR residual serial correlation LM test

Null hypothesis: no serial correlation at lag order h		
Sample: 1980 2014		
Included observations: 33		
Lags	LM-Stat	Probability
1	38.88366	0.3411

Note: Probabilities from chi-square with 36 degrees of freedom

Table 4.5 VAR residual heteroskedasticity test

Cross terms (only levels and squares)		
Sample: 1980 2014		
Included observations: 33		
Joint test:		
Chi-sq	Degrees of freedom	Probability
276.4619	252	0.1388

Eigenvalue statistic show that there are six eigenvalues that are non-zero; this indicates that system as a whole is stationary. So it is not appropriate to model variables in VECM. I, therefore, employed VAR instead of VECM. The reason for not differencing the data is to avoid loss of important information contained in the variables (more detail is given in the econometric methodology section).

In the next step, six variables reduced form VAR has been estimated by OLS and using data in level form. Most of the variables in the model are supposed to be highly persistent, but as discussed in the methodology section, that VAR in level form can be used even if variables are unit root processes. The AIC is minimum at three lags, while SIC is minimum at first lag of the VAR. The likelihood ratio (LR) test also recommends one lag. Therefore, only one lag is included in the VAR model (see Table 4.3 for details).

Some diagnostic tests have been employed to analyze behaviour of the residual series. The multivariate LM test is used and results (in Table 4.4) show that there is no autocorrelation in the residuals. This shows that appropriate number of lags have been chosen. Moreover, the residuals are found to be identically distributed, as shown from results of multivariate White test for heteroskedasticity[19] (see

[19] See White (1980) for details.

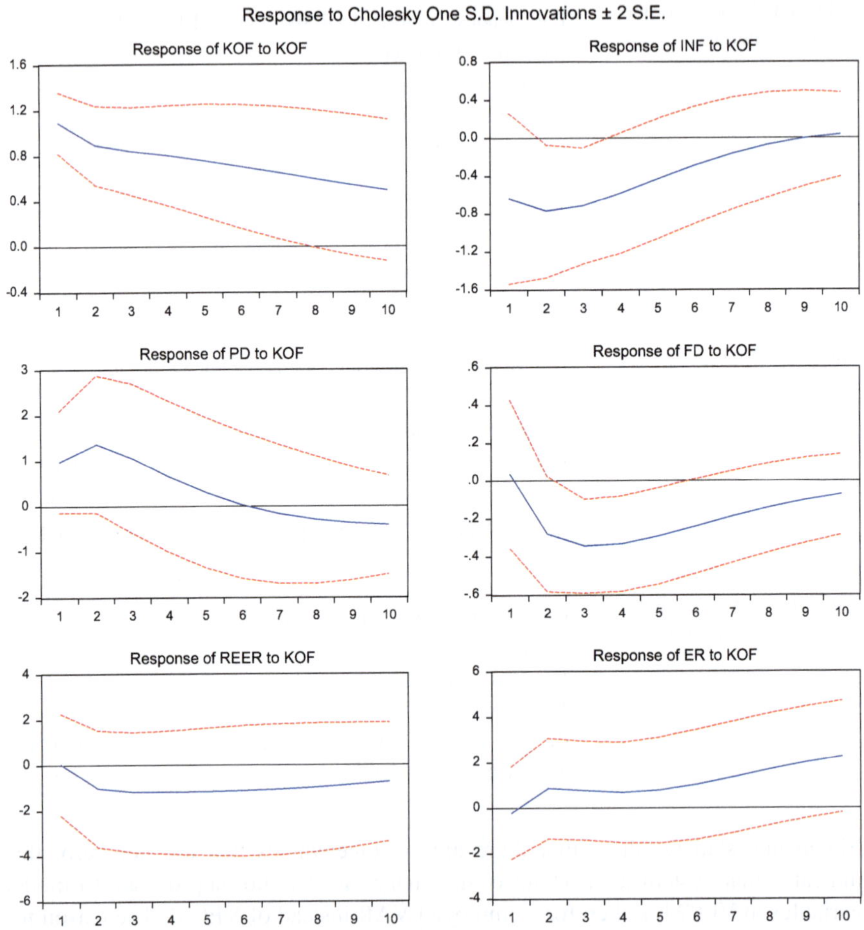

Note: Solid line indicates impulse response function, while the two dotted lines are representative of +/- 2 standard error or 95% confidence interval.

Fig. 4.1 VAR Simulations of KOF index of globalization on components of MII. *Note*: *Solid line* indicates impulse response function, while the *two dotted lines* are representative of +/− 2 standard error or 95 % confidence interval

Table 4.5). This indicates that the variables do not follow multivariate ARCH process, therefore, VAR model is appropriate for the analysis. Results of reduced form VAR are given in Table 4.8. Moreover, the above stated restrictions are imposed to recover structural shocks (results of structural parameters are given in Table 4.9). However, only impulse response functions have been provided here, which show relationship among variables of the system.

The impulse response of KOF index of globalization (abbreviated as KOF) on itself highlights the presence of path dependence, and the persistence of the series. It is shown in Fig. 4.1 that the positive shock in KOF remains persistent for around

7 years. The series of KOF has long memory as the lagged effect remains significant for about 7 years.

In the case of inflation, one standard deviation (SD) positive shock of KOF reduces inflation rate immediately. The impulse response further indicates that the shock impacts with a time lag of around 1 year. This effect reaches its peak (trough in the figure) in second year after the shock and the effect remains significant for 2 years after the shock. Although the negative effect remains there till the seventh year but it becomes insignificant in the fourth year. Similarly, the positive shock of KOF, negatively impacts FD, with a time lag of around 1 year. The impulse response indicates that the impact is most profound for 2–5 years after the shock, and it becomes insignificant after 6 years.

The impact of increase in KOF index on public debt is positive, but it is statistically insignificant. The reason for this result is that KOF has effect on debt only through fiscal deficit. Hence, the effect of KOF on debt is insignificant after controlling for the effect of KOF index on fiscal deficit. Similarly, the impact on real effective exchange rate and nominal exchange rate is found to be statistically insignificant.

Despite insignificant effect of KOF index on some of the sub-indices of MII, further analysis has been conducted on all sub-indices of MII. It may be the case that individual effect of variables is insignificant but their joint effect is significant. Therefore, we have estimated another VAR system in which effect of KOF on overall MII has been traced out.

4.5.2 VAR and Impulse Response Functions of MII, Real GDP and KOF Index of Globalization

I have estimated three variables VAR comprising of log values of real GDP, MII and KOF index of globalization, for counterfactual simulation of growth rate of real GDP. The objective is to capture the direct and indirect relationship between KOF index and GDP. Results in Fig. 4.2 indicate that KOF index has persistent effect on itself and the effect dies out after 5 years. Interestingly, KOF index positively responds to GDP but MII does not affect IQ. Actually, log values of real GDP reflect both long term growth and short term deviations from trend path, whereas MII indicates only short term instability. Institutions are developed over the long run; that's why long run growth in GDP has a significant effect on IQ.

The MII negatively responds to KOF index; the effect is at its peak after 1 year but it gradually dies out to zero after 5 years. This result is consistent with that of the last section, which indicates its robustness. The effect of MII on itself is positive but it has less inertia in that the effect is significant only for 1 year after the shock. The real GDP does not affect MII as the latter is only short run phenomenon, whereas the former is predominantly determined by the long run fundamentals.

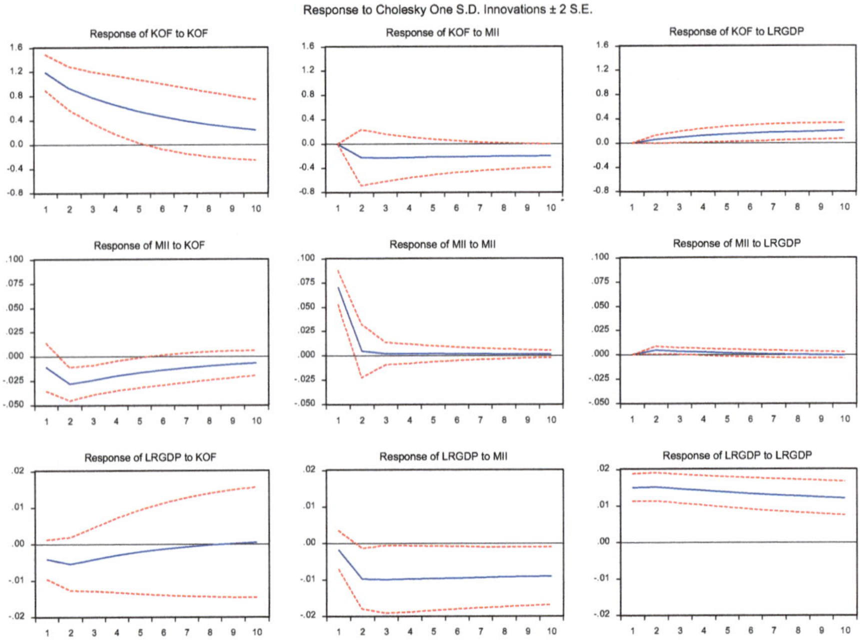

Note: Solid line indicates impulse response function, while the two dotted lines are representative of +/- 2 standard error or 95% confidence interval.

Fig. 4.2 Impulse response functions. *Note*: *Solid line* indicates impulse response function, while the *two dotted lines* are representative of +/− 2 standard error or 95 % confidence interval

Finally and more interestingly, the direct effect of KOF index on GDP is found to be insignificant but MII does affect GDP even in the long run. This result validates the main hypothesis that institutional quality dampens macroeconomic instability, which provides enabling environment for achieving higher growth rate of real GDP. Moreover, this result justifies the suggestion that IMF can play an important role in the short term stabilization, as well as in the long run growth by making its programme conditional on improving determinants of IQ.

4.5.3 Simulations

Counterfactual Simulation Results As mentioned above, under the traditional approach IMF focuses primarily on stabilization and growth, and not much on institutions. However, as found in Chap. 3, institutional quality has significant effect on macroeconomic instability, which in turn affects economic growth. The current chapter, therefore, deals with counterfactual analysis by developing a hypothetical case in which IMF imposes conditionality of improving institutional quality determinants (KOF index in this case) by a certain percentage, and then the

Table 4.6 Comparison of actual and historically simulated figures

	MII		RGDP
	Average	SD	Growth rate
Actual	0.4425	0.1066	4.63
Low scenario	0.4146	0.1030	5.08
Moderate scenario	0.3952	0.1026	5.37
High scenario	0.3836	0.1043	5.57

effects of this intervention on macroeconomic variables are estimated. Through these variables MII is constructed and average value of MII and its variance are compared with that of the actual data. The intervention is effective if it reduces MII compared to what has been found in actual data. The same is done for growth rate of real GDP.

Historical Simulations The economic system is assumed as described by VAR in the last section. In the simulation analysis, data on all sub-indices of MII are supposed to be generated through estimated VAR and estimated shocks. However, for counterfactual analysis, hypothetical cases are assumed in which IMF imposes conditionalities to improve KOF index. For this, three scenarios are assumed with respect to improvement in KOF index; low scenario corresponds to 5 % improvement in KOF index, moderate scenario corresponds to 10 % improvement, while high scenario corresponds to 15 % improvement in KOF index. Results are given in Table 4.6.

Results are in conformity with the hypothesis that improvement in institutional quality will reduce macroeconomic instability, and increase GDP growth rate. In all the three hypothetical scenarios average value of MII is less than that found in actual data. And this effect increases with increase in the improvement in KOF index. The standard deviation (SD) also decreases with increase in KOF index, but the relationship is opposite for 15 % increase in KOF. The GDP growth rate also increases as institutional quality improves, and the gain is quite significant. It may be pointed that the economy of Pakistan, on average, grew by 5 % over the last five decades.[20] However, the results here show that this average growth rate could have been increased to above 5 % by improving IQ. The IMF programmes intend to stabilize the economy in the short run, which positively contributes to high growth in the long run. Results here clearly point to the fact that this objective can be better achieved through positive intervention regarding IQ.

Stochastic Simulations Although results of historical simulations are according to the hypothesis assumed, but these results are less reliable as these are based on only one time simulations, whereby historically observed shocks are assumed to be the only shocks that can disturb the system. However, shocks series follow random process and need not remain same in the future. Had a different shock series been

[20] Calculation on the basis of various issues of Pakistan's Economic Survey (http://www.finance.gov.pk/).

Table 4.7 Comparison of actual and stochastically simulated figures

	MII		RGDP
	Average	SD	Growth rate
Actual	0.443	0.107	0.046
Low scenario	0.436	0.103	0.050
P-value	*(0.600)*		*(0.700)*
Moderate scenario	0.427	0.106	0.051
P-value	*(0.680)*		*(0.790)*
High scenario	0.416	0.109	0.053
P-value	*(0.720)*		*(0.890)*

observed, different simulation results would have been achieved. To check the robustness of the results, therefore, stochastic simulation analysis has been conducted, whereby 10,000 different scenarios have been built-in with respect to shocks for each of the series in the VAR model. As the actual probability density function of structural shocks is unknown, therefore, bootstrap procedure has been employed to check the reliability of the estimates. In 10,000 repetitions, average values of the parameters, along with the values of probability have been indicated in Table 4.7.

Results of stochastic simulation are broadly in conformity with those found in historical simulations. Average value and standard deviation of MII decrease, and real GDP growth rate increases in response to increase in the value of KOF index. However, the difference between actual and average value of MII is smaller compared to that in the case of historical simulation. But in the case of growth rate results remain almost the same. It has also been found that the probability, that increased KOF index by 5 % will result in lower value of MII than the actual value, is 0.60, and the probability of growth rate being higher than the actual one is 0.70. The corresponding probabilities for 10 % increase in KOF index are 0.68 and 0.79, and for 15 % increase are 0.72 and 0.89, respectively.

4.6 Conclusion

The objective of this paper was to estimate the effect of improvement in a significant determinant of institutional quality, KOF Index of Globalization, on macroeconomic instability and real economic growth, in the case of a prolonged user of IMF resources, Pakistan. For this purpose, a VAR model has been estimated and counterfactual analysis has been done both through historical-, as well as stochastic simulation using bootstrap procedure.

Results indicate that macroeconomic instability can be reduced and hence higher growth rate of GDP can be achieved through intervention regarding institutional quality. The IMF, therefore, can achieve its objectives of bringing macroeconomic stabilization and improving economic growth in the recipient country by enhancing the scope of its programme conditionalities to include focus on improving institutional quality.

Appendix

Table 4.8 Reduced form VAR estimates

	KOF	INF	PD	FD	REER	ER
KOF(−1)	0.832827	−0.344534	0.410864	−0.196542	−0.729452	1.370356
	(0.10673)	(0.25628)	(0.31951)	(0.11007)	(0.62944)	(0.56841)
	[7.80299]	[−1.34437]	[1.28592]	[−1.78554]	[−1.15889]	[2.41086]
INF(−1)	0.083740	0.161666	0.058166	0.000356	0.337445	0.171875
	(0.06893)	(0.16552)	(0.20635)	(0.07109)	(0.40652)	(0.36711)
	[1.21481]	[0.97672]	[0.28187]	[0.00501]	[0.83008]	[0.46819]
PD(−1)	0.051135	−0.288177	0.909026	−0.073867	0.043610	−0.424193
	(0.03983)	(0.09564)	(0.11924)	(0.04108)	(0.23491)	(0.21213)
	[1.28375]	[−3.01305]	[7.62349]	[−1.79815]	[0.18565]	[−1.99969]
FD(−1)	−0.232726	0.064702	1.470691	0.370875	−1.542596	1.465871
	(0.19138)	(0.45953)	(0.57291)	(0.19737)	(1.12864)	(1.01921)
	[−1.21604]	[0.14080]	[2.56706]	[1.87905]	[−1.36677]	[1.43824]
REER(−1)	−0.016746	−0.127285	0.061975	−0.027921	0.846542	−0.03486
	(0.01507)	(0.03619)	(0.04512)	(0.01554)	(0.08888)	(0.08027)
	[−1.11105]	[−3.51712]	[1.37361]	[−1.79629]	[9.52403]	[−0.43430]
ER(−1)	0.011252	0.009456	−0.046351	0.011600	0.128253	0.735696
	(0.01655)	(0.03975)	(0.04956)	(0.01707)	(0.09763)	(0.08816)
	[0.67971]	[0.23789]	[−0.93529]	[0.67941]	[1.31367]	[8.34467]
C	6.296581	53.82670	−24.42592	19.19467	40.40490	−12.82334
	(6.93364)	(16.6488)	(20.7563)	(7.15078)	(40.8904)	(36.9258)
	[0.90812]	[3.23307]	[−1.17679]	[2.68428]	[0.98813]	[−0.34727]
R-squared	0.988513	0.547322	0.883402	0.630514	0.971136	0.986238
Adj. R-squared	0.985862	0.442857	0.856495	0.545248	0.964475	0.983062
Sum sq. residuals	31.12421	179.4484	278.9180	33.10408	1082.473	882.7434

(continued)

Table 4.8 (continued)

	KOF	INF	PD	FD	REER	ER
S.E. equation	1.094114	2.627139	3.275304	1.128377	6.452410	5.826806
F-statistic	372.9071	5.239321	32.83143	7.394681	145.7962	310.5398
Log likelihood	−45.85936	−74.76574	−82.04274	−46.87693	−104.4182	−101.0527
Akaike AIC	3.203598	4.955500	5.396530	3.265269	6.752616	6.548647
Schwarz SC	3.521039	5.272941	5.713971	3.582710	7.070057	6.866088
Mean dependent	40.99879	8.117518	63.97838	6.152457	121.3252	70.18091
S.D. dependent	9.201787	3.519654	8.646054	1.673274	34.23384	44.77123
Determinant residual covariance (d.o.f. adj.)		43745.19				
Determinant residual covariance		10463.74				
Log likelihood		−433.6684				
Akaike information criterion		28.82839				
Schwarz criterion		30.73303				

Table 4.9 Structural VAR estimates

Model: Ae = Bu where E[uu′] = I

Restriction type: short-run text form

@e1 = C(1)*@u1

@e2 = C(2)*@e1 + C(3)*@u2

@e3 = C(4)*@e1 + C(5)*@e2 + C(6)*@u3

@e4 = C(7)*@e1 + C(8)*@e2 + C(9)*@e3 + C(10)*@u4

@e5 = C(11)*@e1 + C(12)*@e2 + C(13)*@e3 + C(14)*@e4 + C(15)*@u5

@e6 = C(16)*@e1 + C(17)*@e2 + C(18)*@e3 + C(19)*@e4 + C(20)*@e5 + C(21)*@u6

where

@e1 represents KOF residuals

@e2 represents INF residuals

@e3 represents PD residuals

@e4 represents FD residuals

@e5 represents REER residuals

@e6 represents ER residuals

	Coefficient	Std. error	z-Statistic	Prob.	
C(2)	−0.580125	0.405605	−1.430271	0.1526	
C(4)	0.738795	0.498194	1.482948	0.1381	
C(5)	−0.28273	0.207481	−1.362682	0.1730	
C(7)	−0.134006	0.162886	−0.8227	0.4107	
C(8)	0.004184	0.067506	0.061978	0.9506	
C(9)	0.189271	0.055108	3.434514	0.0006	
C(11)	1.136556	0.942127	1.206372	0.2277	
C(12)	0.316773	0.386531	0.819528	0.4125	
C(13)	−1.014007	0.367620	−2.758303	0.0058	
C(14)	0.149785	0.996693	0.150281	0.8805	

(continued)

Table 4.9 (continued)

C(16)	0.091603	0.814270	0.112497	0.9104	
C(17)	0.389208	0.330253	1.178516	0.2386	
C(18)	−0.153706	0.344935	−0.445608	0.6559	
C(19)	2.836657	0.843330	3.363638	0.0008	
C(20)	−0.218868	0.147242	−1.486458	0.1372	
C(1)	1.094114	0.134676	8.124038	0.0000	
C(3)	2.549311	0.313799	8.124038	0.0000	
C(6)	3.038486	0.374012	8.124038	0.0000	
C(10)	0.961906	0.118402	8.124038	0.0000	
C(15)	5.507458	0.677921	8.124038	0.0000	
C(21)	4.658421	0.573412	8.124038	0.0000	
Log likelihood	−457.2711				
Estimated A matrix					
1.000000	0.000000	0.000000	0.000000	0.000000	0.000000
0.580125	1.000000	0.000000	0.000000	0.000000	0.000000
−0.738795	0.282730	1.000000	0.000000	0.000000	0.000000
0.134006	−0.004184	−0.189271	1.000000	0.000000	0.000000
−1.136556	−0.316773	1.014007	−0.149785	1.000000	0.000000
−0.091603	−0.389208	0.153706	−2.836657	0.218868	1.000000
Estimated B matrix:					
1.094114	0.000000	0.000000	0.000000	0.000000	0.000000
0.000000	2.549311	0.000000	0.000000	0.000000	0.000000
0.000000	0.000000	3.038486	0.000000	0.000000	0.000000
0.000000	0.000000	0.000000	0.961906	0.000000	0.000000
0.000000	0.000000	0.000000	0.000000	5.507458	0.000000
0.000000	0.000000	0.000000	0.000000	0.000000	4.658421

References

Acemoglu D (2006) A simple model of inefficient institutions. Scand J Econ 108:515–546
Acemoglu D, Johnson S (2005) Unbundling institutions. J Polit Econ 113:949–995
Acemoglu D, Robinson J (2001) A theory of political transitions. Am Econ Rev 91:938–963
Acemoglu D, Robinson JA (2006) De facto political power and institutional persistence. Am Econ Assoc 96:325–330
Acemoglu D, Robinson JA (2008) Persistence of power, elites, and institutions. Am Econ Rev 98:267–293
Acemoglu D, Robinson JA (2012) Why nations fail: the origins of power, prosperity, and poverty, 1st edn. Crown Business, New York, NY
Acemoglu D, Johnson S, Robinson J, Thaicharoen Y (2003) Institutional causes, macroeconomic symptoms: volatility, crises and growth. J Monet Econ 50:49–123
Afonso A, Jalles JT (2011) Economic performance and government size. ECB working paper series No. 1399, ECB, Germany
Ahmad E, Mohammed A (2012) Pakistan, the United States and the IMF: great game or a curious case of Dutch disease without the oil? Asia Research Centre working paper no 57. London School of Economics, London, UK
Bernanke B (1986) Alternative explorations of the money-income correlations. In K Brunner, AH Meltzer (eds) Real business cycles, real exchange rates, and actual policies. Carnegie-Rochester Conference Series on Public Policy No. 25, pp 123–56
Blanchard OJ, Quah D (1989) The dynamic effects of aggregate demand and supply disturbances. Am Econ Rev 79:655–673
Braun PA, Mittnik S (1993) Misspecifications in vector autoregressions and their effects on impulse responses and variance decompositions. J Econ 59:319–341
Commons JR (1931) Institutional economics. Am Econ Rev 21:648–657
Cooley TF, LeRoy SF (1985) Atheoretical macroeconomics: a critique. J Monet Econ 16 (3):283–308
Dornbusch R (1976) Expectations and exchange rate dynamics. J Polit Econ 84:1161–1176
Enders W (2015) Applied econometric time series, 4th edn. Wiley, Hoboken, NJ
Garratt AK, Lee MHP, Shin Y (1998) A long run structural macroeconometric model of the UK, Department of Applied Economics Working Paper. University of Cambridge, Cambridge
Groenewegen J, Spithoven A, van den Berg A (2010) Institutional economics: an introduction, 1st edn. Palgrave Macmillan, Hampshire
Hafer RW, Sheehan RG (1991) Policy inference using VAR models. Econ Inq 29:44–52
Haghighi AK, Sameti M, Isfahani RD (2012) The effect of macroeconomic instability on economic growth in Iran. Res Appl Econ 4(3):9–61
Hussain I (1999) Pakistan: the economy of an elitist state, 1st edn. Oxford University Press, Karachi
IEO/IMF (2002) Report of the Independent Evaluation Office (IEO) on prolonged use of IMF resources. IMF, Washington, DC
Ismihan M (2003) The role of politics and instability and public spending dynamics and macroeconomic performance: theory and evidence from Turkey, PhD thesis. METU, Ankara
Kemal AR (2003) Institutional change, growth, and poverty levels in Pakistan. Pak Dev Rev 42:299–311
Khan MS, Knight MD (1985) Fund supported adjustment programs and economic growth. IMF Occasional papers No. 41. IMF, Washington, DC
Khawaja MI, Khan S (2009) Reforming institutions: where to begin? Pakistan Inst Dev Econ Work Pap 50:1–27
Khawaja I, Khan S (2011) Predation, institutional quality and economic growth. Pak Dev Rev 50:809–820
Killick T (1995) IMF programmes in developing countries: design and effects, 1st edn. Routledge, London

Leamer EE (1985) Vector autoregressions for causal inference? Carn-Roch Ser Public Policy 22:255–304

Libecap GD (1989) Distributional issues in contracting for property rights. J Inst Theor Econ 145:6–24

Lütkepohl H (1991) Introduction to multiple time series analysis. Springer, Berlin

North DC (1994) Economic performance through time. Am Econ Rev 84:359–368

Oge Guney P (2007) Fiscal theory of exchange rate determination: empirical evidence from Turkey. Econ Bull 5:1–12

Polak JJ (1957) Monetary analysis of income formation and payments problems. IMF Staff Pap 6:1–50, IMF, Washington, DC

Sims CA (1980) Macroeconomics and reality. Econometrica 48:1–48

Sims CA (1986) Are forecasting models usable for policy analysis? Federal Reserve Bank of Minneapolis Q Rev 10:1–16

Sims CA (1992) Interpreting the macroeconomic time series facts: the effects of monetary policy. Eur Econ Rev 36:975–1000

Sims CA, Stock JH, Watson MW (1990) Inference in linear time series models with some unit roots. Econometrica 58:113–144

von Hagen J (1991) A note on the empirical effectiveness of formal fiscal restraints. J Public Econ 44:99–110

von Hayek FA (1979) The counter-revolution of science. Studies on the abuse of reason, 2nd edn. Liberty Press, Indianapolis, IN

White H (1980) A heteroskedasticity-consistent covariance matrix estimator and a direct test for heteroskedasticity. Econometrica 48:817–838

Chapter 5
Concluding Remarks

Abstract This book investigates the impact of International Monetary Fund (IMF) programmes on macroeconomic instability and economic growth in recipient countries. Employing the New Institutional Economics approach as an analytical framework, it identifies the determinants of economic and political institutional quality by taking into account a broad variety of indicators such as parliamentary forms of government, the aggregate governance level, civil and economic liberties, property rights etc. The book subsequently estimates the impact of these institutional determinants on real economic growth, both directly and also indirectly, through the channel of macroeconomic instability, in recipient countries. Moreover, by conducting counterfactual analysis it illustrates the impact of enhanced focus of IMF programmes towards improving institutional quality, on the situation of macroeconomic stability and economic growth in the case of Pakistan, a frequent user of IMF resources.

The book is an attempt to explore the importance of determinants of institutional quality on both macroeconomic stability and real economic growth in primarily IMF programme countries.

The changing role of IMF—one from mainly maintaining the par-value system in member countries to provider of financial resources to ever increasing number of countries after the Third World debt crisis—not only enhanced the scope of its activities, but the conditionalities that were imposed had a telling impact on the economic performance of recipient countries. Together with this, there was a rise in the amount of research that started to gauge the performance of these programmes in terms of putting in place an environment that supported sustained macroeconomic stability and real economic growth. Research literature, applying different counterfactual methodologies, pointed towards below par performance of the Fund on both these counts. Hence, overall macroeconomic stability could not be achieved in programme countries on sustained basis (Evrensel 2002; Easterly 2005), with no significant consequence of IMF programmes for either investment or inflation. Also, no positive consequence on economic growth in recipient countries could be found (Barro and Lee 2005). At the same time, many countries (including Pakistan) became prolonged users of IMF resources.

Similar consequences raised alarm among many researchers on the underlying Neo-Classical/Monetarist behavioural assumptions of IMF programmes, who

O. Javed, *The Economic Impact of International Monetary Fund Programmes*, Contributions to Economics, DOI 10.1007/978-3-319-29178-9_5

found them as too rigid, and not context-specific. The main problem was that IMF, as against the demand side of the economy, did not put adequate emphasis on the supply side. Even when it did internalize this criticism to some extent, the behavioural underpinnings of its programmes did not allow it to understand the due importance of institutions for macroeconomic stability and economic growth.

On the other hand, NIE saw economic agents as having bounded rationality, and who were faced with transaction costs in a world of asymmetric information. Hence, they saw improvement in institutional quality as important for reducing costs faced by agents in the economy, and in turn overall had a positive impact on economic growth (Rodrik et al. 2002; Hall and Jones 1999). A closer look indicated that institutions helped evolve such governance structures that caused reduction in transaction costs (Groenewegen et al. 2010). According to NIE literature, both political- and economic institutions existed, where one influenced the other to bring overall change in institutional quality (Acemoglu 2006; Acemoglu and Robinson 2008, 2012). The current study is therefore motivated by this 'missing link of institutions' in IMF programmes.

The framework of NIE gives importance to both the political and economic determinants of institutional quality. In Chap. 2, important determinants of institutional quality are researched in literature. Thereafter, they are tested for significance to reach important determinants of institutional quality among them. The scope of the study is primarily the IMF programme countries, while a special analysis is also extended to see which determinants are particularly significant in the case of prolonged users. Among the various proxy variables for political- and economic institutional quality (PIQ and EIQ), respectively, the ones employed are Economic Freedom Index (EFI) of the Cato Institute[1] for EIQ, and Polity II (from the Polity IV dataset of Marshall et al. 2011), which captures 'political structures and regime change'[2] for PIQ.

Selection of time period was important, and it was appropriate to select the starting point around the time of the Third World debt crisis, because it was then that the quantity and country coverage of IMF programmes substantially increased. Moreover, in order to make proper identification of prolonged users, it was important to have 10 years of time periods. Hence, to achieve reliable results, 1980–2009 (30 years) was selected as appropriate time period.

A number of institutional determinants were identified from literature as potentially important institutional determinants that covered both the political/governance related sphere and also economic dimension. The variables on the political side included, type of regime indicating the presence of either presidential or parliamentary form of government, chief executive a military officer or not, the strength of government and opposition in parliament (indicated by Herfindahl Indices) respectively, quality of overall governance level, and extent of civil

[1] http://www.cato.org/economic-freedom-world

[2] http://www.icpsr.umich.edu/icpsrweb/ICPSR/studies/9263?q=Polity IIandsearchSource=icpsr-landing

liberties. On the economic side, extent of openness (indicated by KOF Index of Globalization, taken as a proxy variable), measures of monetary-, fiscal-, and investment freedom, property rights, and real GDP were taken.

A panel of 129 IMF programme countries were taken, and by applying the System GMM approach, results indicated that the dynamic process is highly persistent for both economic- and political institutional quality, highlighting the aspect of path dependent nature of evolution of institutional quality. Estimation results indicated that, a parliamentary form of government, level of aggregate governance, extent of civil liberties, level of openness, and property rights all have a positive impact on overall institutional quality. Separately both monetary- and investment freedom enhance political institutional quality; while economic growth positively impacts economic institutional quality. Moreover, military in power reduces political institutional quality. Hence, it could be seen that institutional determinants matter for the way political and economic institutions evolve in IMF programme countries. Also, improved institutional determinants help provide an environment for better policy implementation, something important for execution of an IMF programme and its successful completion.

Chapter 3 started with identifying the criticism of IMF programmes in literature, which called for a rethinking of IMF programmes in terms of its behaviourial assumptions, and the rigid and one-size-fits-all kind of approach. With this context serving as a motivation, significant institutional determinants (from the previous chapter) are then tested- using a panel of IMF programme countries (in terms of prolonged and non-prolonged users), and by applying once again the System GMM approach- on real economic growth, to see in turn their impact for time duration of 1980–2009. Subsequently, the estimated impact of institutional determinants (both political and economic) was found to be overall significant for enhancing real economic growth, both for prolonged- and non-prolonged users of IMF.

Along with looking at the direct impact of institutional determinants on real economic growth, their impact was also checked on macroeconomic instability. Moreover, here the indirect impact of institutional determinants on real economic growth was also seen through the channel of macroeconomic stability. Results indicated that in fact such a relationship did exist, whereby institutional determinants positively impacted real GDP both directly, as well as indirectly, through the channel of macroeconomic stability. As an extension, similar results were obtained for non-programme countries, in terms of both the direct and indirect impact of institutional determinants on real economic growth.

In Chap. 4, representative prolonged user in the shape of Pakistan was focused upon with the underlying motivation to explore the importance of institutional quality determinants for both macroeconomic stability and real economic growth here. Moreover, a detailed analysis was also presented to bring understanding of the overall institutional landscape of Pakistan, the role of political- and economic elites, and the impact of IMF programmes in particular, and overall policy in general. The analysis was made from the perspective of NIE, and suggestions about evolving a more efficient institutional matrix and incentive system, along with governance structures were also laid out.

As indicated, Pakistan was selected among the prolonged users as a representative case study, because even after having been in many IMF programmes since the 1980s (being a prolonged user in both the decades of 1990s and 2000s), it had not been able to achieve either sustained macroeconomic stabilization or real economic growth. For meeting the technical requirement of VAR analysis technique, the time duration was expanded by taking a period of 1980–2014, while the institutional quality determinant that was suited for analytical purpose (under this technique) was chosen to be KOF index of globalization.

Here, time series data of Pakistan was backcasted to see the impact of enhanced institutional focus on macroeconomic instability and economic growth. For analysis, VAR (Vector Autoregression) was constructed using all sub-indices of MII and indices of institutional quality—KOF index of globalization. Thereafter, appropriate restrictions were imposed on contemporaneous relationship of variables to make VAR identified and for recovering structural shocks; which were then used to trace out the effect of KOF index of globalization on sub-indices of MII, and real economic growth, respectively. Thereafter, counterfactual simulations were conducted, assuming a hypothetical situation in which IMF programme has an institutional focus, whereby low, moderate, and high scenarios were taken in terms of 5 %, 10 %, and 15 % enhancements in KOF index of globalization, respectively. The thought process behind this was to see how gradual improvement in institutional quality impacted macroeconomic instability and real economic growth.

Results indicated that intervention whereby institutional quality was enhanced, reduced macroeconomic instability and increased GDP growth rate. In all the three hypothetical scenarios, average value of MII was less than that found in actual data; while this effect increased with increasing improvement in KOF index. It was pointed out that through enhanced institutional focus by IMF programmes, Pakistan's economy could have grown more that its average economic growth of 5 % during the last five decades.

It is therefore being advised that IMF programmes put greater focus on institutional quality determinants so that they can perform better in terms of their objectives of achieving sustained macroeconomic stability and economic growth, both for the programme countries in general, and prolonged users in particular.

References

Acemoglu D (2006) A simple model of inefficient institutions. Scand J Econ 108:515–546

Acemoglu D, Robinson JA (2008) Persistence of power, elites, and institutions. Am Econ Rev 98:267–293

Acemoglu D, Robinson JA (2012) Why nations fail: the origins of power, prosperity, and poverty, 1st edn. Crown Business, New York, NY

Barro RJ, Lee J (2005) IMF programs: who is chosen and what are the effects? J Monet Econ 52:1245–1269

Easterly W (2005) What did structural adjustment adjust? The association of policies and growth with repeated IMF and World Bank adjustment loans. J Dev Econ 76:1–22

Evrensel AY (2002) Effectiveness of IMF-supported stabilization programmes in developing countries. J Int Money Finance 21:565–587

Groenewegen J, Spithoven A, van den Berg A (2010) Institutional economics: an introduction, 1st edn. Palgrave Macmillan, Hampshire

Hall RE, Jones CI (1999) Why do some countries produce so much more output per worker than others? Q J Econ 114:83–116

Marshall MG, Jaggers K, Gurr TR (2011) Polity IV Project: dataset users' manual. Polity IV Project, Arlington, VA

Rodrik D, Subramanian A, Trebbi F (2002) Institutions rule: the primacy of institutions over geography and integration in economic development. Centre for Economic Policy Research Discussion paper series no 3643. Centre for Economic Policy Research, London

MIX
Papier aus verantwortungsvollen Quellen
Paper from responsible sources
FSC® C105338

If you have any concerns about our products,
you can contact us on
ProductSafety@springernature.com

In case Publisher is established outside the EU,
the EU authorized representative is:
Springer Nature Customer Service Center GmbH
Europaplatz 3, 69115 Heidelberg, Germany

Printed by Libri Plureos GmbH
in Hamburg, Germany